Elizabethan Marlowe

Elizabethan
Marlowe

*Writing and Culture in the English
Renaissance*

WILLIAM ZUNDER

Unity Press

First published 1994 by
Unity Press Limited
34 Canongate
Cottingham
Hull   HU16 4DG

British Library Cataloguing - in - Publication Data
A catalogue record for this book is
available from the British Library

ISBN 0 9523180 0 8

Typeset in 11pt Times by
Gem DTP, Elloughton
Printed and bound in Great Britain by
CPU, Hull University

To
Thomas, Harriet, Charlotte, and Prudence
carissima pignora

Contents

Preface   9

Chapter 1   Life and Context   11

Chapter 2   *Tamburlaine*: Empire and Stoicism   14

Chapter 3   The *Jew of Malta*: Policy and Greed   31

Chapter 4   *Edward II*: Power and Love   44

Chapter 5   *Doctor Faustus*: Science and Religion   62

Chapter 6   *Hero and Leander*: Love and Fate   76

Notes   92

Index   107

Contents

Preface

This book is intended as a discussion of Marlowe suitable for students. At the same time, it is offered as an original contribution in its own right. It is written from a broadly historicist position.[1]

I have kept annotation to a minimum. The secondary material on Marlowe is extensive, and has been reviewed by William Tydeman and Vivien Thomas, *State of the Art: Christopher Marlowe* (Bristol, 1989). And the notes register specific debts or particular disagreements, or function as suggestions for further reading. Dates of composition, nearly always a problem in the sixteenth century, are taken in most instances from standard editions. In the case of Marlowe, these are: *Dido Queen of Carthage and The Massacre at Paris: Christopher Marlowe*, edited by H.J. Oliver (London, 1968); *Tamburlaine the Great: Christopher Marlowe*, edited by J.S. Cunningham (Manchester, 1981); *The Jew of Malta: Christopher Marlowe*, edited by N.W. Bawcutt (Manchester, 1978); *Edward II*, edited by H.B. Charlton and R.D. Waller, second edition, revised by F.N. Lees (London, 1955). With *Doctor Faustus* and *Hero and Leander*, I have relied on *Doctor Faustus: Christopher Marlowe*, edited by John D. Jump, revised edition (London, 1965), and *The Poems: Christopher Marlowe*, edited by Millar Maclure (London, 1968); but have also consulted *The Complete Works of Christopher Marlowe*, edited by Roma Gill, Volumes I-II (Oxford, 1987-90), and *Christopher Marlowe's Doctor Faustus*, edited by Michael

Keefer (Peterborough, Ontario, 1991). I have referred to all these editions in the notes simply by the editor's name and abbreviated title. Quotation of Marlowe is from *The Plays of Christopher Marlowe*, edited by Roma Gill (Oxford, 1971), and *Christopher Marlowe: The Complete Poems and Translations*, edited by Stephen Orgel (Harmondsworth, 1971). On occasion, I have silently amended these texts from the standard editions. And the spelling of incidental quotations from sixteenth-century sources has been tacitly modernised.

I am very grateful to my wife, Anne, and to Margaret Elliott for typing this book for me, and to many friends and colleagues for their help and advice. A special debt is owed to my students, whose concerns and responses over the years have helped give the book shape and direction.

Chapter One

Life and Context

Marlowe was born into the second generation of Elizabethan writers: the generation that included Shakespeare and Donne, and which came to consciousness in the late 1580s and early 1590s. Typically of this generation, he was born into the urban middle class. Born in February 1564, he was the son of a Canterbury shoemaker. Typical, too, was his humanist education. In 1578 he gained a scholarship at King's School, Canterbury; and in 1580, a further scholarship at Corpus Christi College, Cambridge. Four years later he received his BA, and in 1587 his MA; and, by virtue of his university education, moved into the ranks of the gentry. In this social rising, by means of individual ability, he is again characteristic of his generation. As John Bakeless says of him, about the time he left Cambridge he was 'a university man, known to be of humble origin, whose talents [had] made him a reputation', and who is 'ordinarily referred to as "Christopher Marlowe, gentleman"'.[1] It was probably while at Cambridge that he acquired the patronage of Thomas Walsingham, a cousin of Sir Francis Walsingham, the head of Elizabeth's secret service. And it was while at Cambridge that he undertook confidential work for Elizabeth's government. As a result, his opinions came under

official suspicion, at the university, of catholicism.   And it was
only because the privy council vouched for his acceptability that
he was allowed to proceed to his MA.   In a letter dated 29 June
1587, the council assured the university that 'in all his actions he
had behaved himself orderly and discreetly whereby he had done
her majesty good service, and deserved to be rewarded for his
faithful dealing'; and that 'it was not her majesty's pleasure that
anyone employed as he had been in matters touching the benefit
of his country should be defamed by those that are ignorant in
th'affairs he went about'.[2]   Such incorporation of rising talent
into the state structure was not uncommon at the end of the
sixteenth century.   It was characteristic, for example, in their
different ways, of both Shakespeare and Donne.[3]

After Cambridge, Marlowe moved to London.   In 1589 he
was involved in the killing of William Bradley by Thomas
Watson, another dependant of Walsingham's.   And he spent some
time in Newgate prison for this.   In January 1592 he was probably
on government business in Flushing, when he was sent home by
the governor to Lord Burghley, Elizabeth's high treasurer, on a
charge of forgery.   He had been informed against by Richard
Baines, himself a government agent, who also accused him of
intending to defect to the Spanish or Rome.   Marlowe responded
by making the same accusations against him.   Exactly what the
outcome of this was for Marlowe is unknown.   But in May of the
same year he was bound over to keep the peace in Shoreditch.
And in September he took part in a fight with William Corkine in
Canterbury.   Once more, it is likely he was in Canterbury on
government service.   Eight months after that, on 18 May 1593, he
was summoned by the privy council, probably from Scadbury,
Walsingham's country house in Chislehurst, accused of holding
dangerous ideas.   A report of these was compiled around this time
by Marlowe's fellow agent, Baines.   Marlowe answered the
summons on May 20.   And ten days later, he was killed in a
quarrel about the bill in Eleanor Bull's house in Deptford by
Ingram Frizer, another of Walsingham's dependants.   It was a

violent end to a turbulent moment in Marlowe's life: a violence and turbulence not untypical of the time.[4]

The England that Marlowe was born into, and which shaped his life and work, was undergoing radical change. Fundamentally, there was the rise of capitalism. At the beginning of the sixteenth century, England was no longer a feudal society. By the last decades of the century – the 1580s and 90s – it was emerging as a capitalist society. Intertwined with this were other developments. There was the rise of humanism, and the secularisation of education. There was the rise of protestantism, and the disengagement from continental Europe, in particular the confrontation with catholic Spain. There was the rise of nationalism, and the growth of a strong, centralised state, focused on the monarch. There was the rise of parliament; the beginnings of English imperialism; and the rise of science.[5]

Although England was changing, however, the dominant ideology of the time continued to stress the principles of the previous age: the feudal notions of hierarchy, authority, and obedience. The main vehicles for this were the *Homilies*, required to be read every Sunday and holy day in church since 1547, and the *Book of Common Prayer*, used exclusively since its institution in 1549 — in each case, with a brief intermission under Mary. There was, then, a deep contradiction within Elizabethan culture between the dominant discourse, which stressed order and stability, and people's experience which, however enmeshed with it, was becoming increasingly fluid.[6]

Marlowe's career was brief. It lasted no more than six years. But it was brilliant, and highly successful. And it articulated the concerns of the age in a way that had not been done before. This articulation forms the substance of the chapters that follow.

Chapter Two

Tamburlaine: Empire and Stoicism

The first part of *Tamburlaine* was probably written in 1587. Some fifty years earlier, Henry VIII had embarked upon the English reformation. In 1531 he had declared himself head of the church in England. And by the 1580s England was a minor, protestant power, faced by the major state of Europe, catholic Spain. More than faced by, threatened by: in 1585 Spain effectively declared war on England, and three years later attempted a full-scale invasion. The armada years were a moment of great national sentiment. And the emotions generated by the current conflict are displaced onto the action of the play. Behind Tamburlaine, the upstart of central Asia, lies the newly emergent England of Elizabeth. And behind Bajazeth, the emperor of Turkey, lies the overwhelming, imperial power of Spain.[1]

Tamburlaine was an actual historical figure. Born in 1336, he was the son of a Mongol chief. And by the time of his death nearly seventy years later, he had established an empire ranging from Mongolia to the Mediterranean. Marlowe, moreover, turned to what were, for an educated Elizabethan like himself, the most authoritative and recent accounts: the *Life* of Tamburlaine by the Italian humanist, Pietro Perondini, published in 1553, and George Whetstone's *English Mirror*, printed in 1586. Like other works of the renaissance, the play claims the authority of history.[2]

One of the principal emotions articulated by the play is defiance: defiance of foreign power. It is articulated mainly through the character of Tamburlaine himself, who dominates the play's action. These words, for example, to Bajazeth:

> Those walled garrisons will I subdue,
> And write myself great lord of Africa.
> So from the East unto the furthest West
> Shall Tamburlaine extend his puissant arm.
> The galleys and those pilling brigandines,
> That yearly sail to the Venetian gulf,
> And hover in the Straits for Christians' wrack,
> Shall lie at anchor in the Isle Asant,
> Until the Persian fleet and men-of-war,
> Sailing along the oriental sea,
> Have fetch'd about the Indian continent,
> Even from Persepolis to Mexico,
> And thence unto the Straits of Jubalter,
> Where they shall meet and join their force in one,
> Keeping in awe the Bay of Portingale,
> And all the ocean by the British shore;
> And by this means I'll win the world at last.
>
> (Part I, III. 3. 244-60)

The speech is, in fact, an extraordinary assertion of imperial ambition; and is inseparable not only from the conflict with Spain, but also from contemporary English expansion. From voyages of discovery: Cabot to north America, for example, as early as 1497; Willoughby and Chancellor in search of a northeast passage to China in 1553; Frobisher in search of a northwest passage some twenty years later; or Drake's circumnavigation of the world in 1577-80. From attempts at distant colonisation: Virginia in 1585 and 1587. But especially from the conquest and settlement of Ireland. In 1542 Henry VIII had taken the title of king of Ireland. And in the year before the play was written, Munster was colonised.[3]

The conquest of Ireland was extremely brutal; and was not completed until Cromwell crushed the Irish resistance in the mid-seventeenth century. And the play is characterised by the most striking, even exotic, assertions of cruelty. Again, these are made chiefly through Tamburlaine. 'Our conquering swords', he tells Bajazeth:

> shall marshal us the way
> We use to march upon the slaughter'd foe,
> Trampling their bowels with our horses' hoofs,
> Brave horses bred on the white Tartarian hills.
> (Part I, III. 3. 148-51)

And the cruelty is acted out in the drama. There is Tamburlaine's caging of Bajazeth, for instance, or his use of him as a footstool; the gruesome suicides of Bajazeth and Zabina; or the slaughter of the virgins of Damascus, with the image of 'imperious Death' on Tamburlaine's swordpoint, 'keeping his circuit by the slicing edge' (V. 1. 108-12). These events derive from Perondini and Whetstone, and bring with them the discursive power of history. They are presented as fact, not fantasy. But the point to emphasise at this juncture is that, despite the presence of debate in the text — of dialogism — Marlowe endorses the cruelty and the ambition of which it is the instrument. In fact, to judge by the characteristic hyperbole, he revels in it. And to judge by the play's success, he was endorsing a representative trait in the English people of the time.[4]

Marlowe does more than this, however. One of the features of the historical Tamburlaine was his lameness. Perondini says he limped with a 'mis-shapen gait' (*Life*, Chapter 21). Marlowe chooses to ignore this and, instead, picks up Whetstone's contradictory remark about his 'strength and comeliness of . . . body' (*English Mirror*, Book I, Chapter 12). Marlowe not only endorses Tamburlaine. He idealises him. And his description is given not to Zenocrate but to Menaphon, and on a stage peopled entirely by men. He is:

Of stature tall, and straightly fashioned
Like his desire, lift upwards and divine;
So large of limbs, his joints so strongly knit,
Such breadth of shoulders as might mainly bear
Old Atlas' burden.

Around his forehead:

hangs a knot of amber hair,
Wrapped in curls, as fierce Achilles' was,
On which the breath of heaven delights to play,
Making it dance with wanton majesty.
(Part I, II. 1. 7-11, 23-6)[5]

More importantly, Tamburlaine was a member of the ruling class. The historiographical tradition had lost sight of this. Perondini calls him a 'shepherd' (*Life*, Chapter 9 [bis]). And Whetstone refers to him variously as a 'shepherd', a 'labourer', and a 'soldier' (*English Mirror*, Book I, Chapter 12). Marlowe chooses to emphasise this. And there is frequent reference in the play to Tamburlaine's humble origins. The very first words addressed to him immediately place him socially. 'Ah shepherd', says Zenocrate, '(If, as thou seem'st, thou art so mean a man)' (I. 2. 7-8). And Marlowe puts the discourse of feudalism, historically superseded by the early capitalism of the 1580s, into the mouths of his — ineffectual — opponents. The soldan of Egypt, for example, exclaims against him as 'Merciless villain, peasant ignorant / Of lawful arms or martial discipline!' (IV. 1. 64-5).[6]

Tamburlaine's position, of course, is the same as Marlowe's and many of his contemporaries': Shakespeare the son of a glover, Donne the son of an ironmonger. All these rose by the exertion of talent from one class to another; a rise typical of a time when social mobility was becoming familiar, as the new economy dissolved feudal relations. The play involves not only a projection of Marlowe's experience, but also a recognition by the audience of a common situation. For the play's trajectory is the rise of Tamburlaine, solely as the result of natural ability, from a position at the bottom of the social scale to a position at the top. As he declares at the beginning of his rise, 'I am a lord, for so my deeds shall prove, / And yet a shepherd by my parentage' (I. 2. 34-5). The rise is completely successful, despite the momentary disruption of inner doubt in the last scene in the famous apostrophe to Zenocrate ('Ah, fair Zenocrate, divine Zenocrate! / Fair is too foul an epithet for thee . . .': V. 1. 135-91). And the play ends in triumph.[7]

From early in Elizabeth's reign, the metaphor of her marriage to England had been widespread. Spenser had recently reworked it in the *Faerie Queene* where Redcross Knight, representing among other things a questing, protestant England, is betrothed to Una, unitary truth and Elizabeth (I. 12). And the play momentarily condenses this familiar image with the final stage icon, where Tamburlaine latently figures England and Zenocrate, whose name means 'ruler of foreigners', latently figures Elizabeth in a proleptic vision of imperial peace: a Pax Britannica unperturbed by the violence on which it was based — the slaughtered king of Arabia or the grisly corpses of Bajazeth and Zabina, all of whom also form part of the closing tableau (V. 1. 504 to the end). 'And now', says Tamburlaine:

> my lords and loving followers,
> That purchas'd kingdoms by your martial deeds,
> Cast off your armour, put on scarlet robes,
> Mount up your royal places of estate,
> Environed with troops of noblemen,
> And there make laws to rule your provinces.
> Hang up your weapons on Alcides' post,
> For Tamburlaine takes truce with all the world.

Then, turning to Zenocrate:

> Thy first-betrothed love, Arabia,
> Shall we with honour, as beseems, entomb
> With this great Turk and his fair emperess.
> Then, after all these solemn exequies,
> We will our rites of marriage solemnize.
>> (Part I, V. 1. 520 to the end)[8]

Tamburlaine is, in fact, completely resolute. His temporary hesitation in the final scene, induced by Zenocrate's pleading, is emphatically resolved. 'Virtue', he declares, 'solely is the sum of glory, / And fashions men with true nobility' (V. 1. 189-90): 'virtue' in the Machiavellian sense of 'virtù', 'manliness, prowess'. And the play generalises this into an explicit ideology of individualism. It is an individualism that both refuses limit and grounds itself in the contemporary centre of power:

> Nature, that fram'd us of four elements
> Warring within our breasts for regiment,
> Doth teach us all to have aspiring minds.
> Our souls, whose faculties can comprehend
> The wondrous architecture of the world,
> And measure every wand'ring planet's course,
> Still climbing after knowledge infinite,
> And always moving as the restless spheres,
> Wills us to wear ourselves and never rest
> Until we reach the ripest fruit of all,
> That perfect bliss and sole felicity,
> The sweet fruition of an earthly crown.
>> (Part I, II. 7. 18-29)

The speech is delivered by Tamburlaine directly to the audience. And it deliberately challenges the dominant discourse. The *Homily* 'Of Obedience', for example, regularly read out in church and deeply familiar to Marlowe's generation, begins by stressing the

order established by God in nature. And Marlowe's speech is
structured to confront it virtually point by point. The heavens — the
Homily claims — and the earth, in all their plenitude, 'keep their
comely course and order'. Human subjectivity is correspondingly
ordered: 'Man himself . . . hath all his parts both within and
without, as soul, heart, mind, memory, understanding, reason,
speech, with all and singular corporal members of his body, in a
profitable, necessary, and pleasant order'. And the whole discourse
is founded, quite unequivocally, on social and gender hierarchy:

> Every degree of people, in their vocation, calling, and
> office, hath appointed to them their duty and order. Some
> are in high degree, some in low; some kings and princes,
> some inferiors and subjects; priests and laymen, masters
> and servants, fathers and children, husbands and wives,
> rich and poor; and every one have need of other.

Without it, 'all things shall be common; and there must needs
follow all mischief and utter destruction both of souls, bodies,
goods, and commonwealths' (*Two Books of Homilies*, pages 105-6).

The *Homily* continues, moreover, to centre order on the
monarchy, in a politicising turn of thought characteristic of the
dominant view: 'God hath sent us his high gift, our most dear
Sovereign Lady Queen Elizabeth, with godly, wise, and honourable
counsel [that is, the privy council], with other superiors and inferiors,
in a beautiful order and goodly'. Marlowe does not challenge this. In
fact, he intensifies the absolutist tendency of the discourse by
transferring to it the power of traditional religious language. Perfect
'bliss' is to be found not in a heavenly, but an 'earthly' crown (lines 28-
9). The conclusion of the speech is at once surprising and insistent.
At the same time, the refusal of limit subverts the *Homily*'s insistence
on social stasis and on obedience to established authority: 'Let us all
obey, even from the bottom of our hearts, all their godly proceedings,
laws, statutes, proclamations, and injunctions, with all other their
godly orders' (*Two Books of Homilies*, page 106).[9]

It is here perhaps that one can see the kind of reason why, a few years later, the privy council should have had doubts about Marlowe's loyalty. On the one hand, he endorses a vigorous foreign policy, of the kind advocated by Walsingham. But, on the other, he asserts a radical individualism that threatens to undermine the very basis of society as the privy council understood it. The incorporation of Marlowe was not without its tensions and contradictions.

The play, then, constructs a composite and fissile ideology: principally, of imperialism; implicitly, of nationalism; and subversively, of individualism.[10]

There seems no reason to doubt the statement in the prologue to *Tamburlaine*, Part II, that the play was written in response to the commercial success — 'general welcomes' (line 1) — of Part I. Marlowe was, after all, writing for the new, capitalist theatre in London.[11] It would be a mistake, however, to see the play, which Marlowe probably also wrote in 1587, simply as a reworking of the earlier one. The imperialist discourse continues. But the centre of interest shifts. And it focuses, first of all, on deception.

Early in the play, the Hungarians deceive the Turks: the episode of Sigismund and Orcanes. And the play stresses the paradox of the episode: the infidelity of the christians against the fidelity of the muslim infidel. But the paradox is less radical than it might seem. Hungary remained catholic in the sixteenth century. And Marlowe carefully associates the Hungarians' christianity with catholicism. There is the antipapalism of Techelles' reference to Prester John in Act I, Scene 3: 'The mighty Christian priest / Call'd John the Great', 'Whose triple mitre' — the emblem of papal office — 'I did take by force, / And made him swear obedience to my crown' (lines 187-8, 189-90). There is the detailed connection of eastern Europe with Rome at the beginning of the next scene, when Frederick addresses Sigismund:

> Your majesty remembers, I am sure,
> What cruel slaughter of our Christian bloods
> These heath'nish Turks and pagans lately made
> Betwixt the city Zula and Danubius;
> How through the midst of Varna and Bulgaria,
> And almost to the very walls of Rome,
> They have, not long since, massacr'd our camp.
>
> (Part II, II. 1. 4-10)

And there is the classic exposition later in the scene, by Frederick and Baldwin, of the catholic doctrine of equivocation: 'no faith with heretics'. Baldwin speaks of the Turks. But what he says could equally apply to the characteristically protestant London audience:

> with such infidels,
> In whom no faith nor true religion rests,
> We are not bound to those accomplishments
> The holy laws of Christendom enjoin;
> But, as the faith which they profanely plight
> Is not by necessary policy
> To be esteem'd assurance for ourselves,
> So what we vow to them should not infringe
> Our liberty of arms and victory.
>
> (Part II, II. 1. 33-41)

And Frederick clinches the argument: "tis superstition / To stand so strictly on dispensive faith' (II. 1. 49-50) — faith which is subject to papal dispensation.

When Sigismund is defeated in Act II, Scene 3, the action endorses Christ as the punisher of catholic wrongs: as the protestant avenger. As Sigismund says, 'God hath thunder'd vengeance from on high / For my accurs'd and hateful perjury'; God is a 'just and dreadful punisher of sin' (lines 2-3, 4). And this is reinforced through Orcanes, despite the alterity of his notion of

the afterlife which Marlowe carefully constructs for him, largely
out of the koran (lines 18-26); and despite the disruption of
Gazellus's rationalist explanation that Sigismund's defeat was
simply the 'fortune of the wars' (line 31). To Orcanes his defeat
shows the 'justice of his Christ' and Christ's 'power, which here
appears as full / As rays of Cynthia to the clearest sight' (lines 28,
29-30). The episode, in other words, is not antichristian or
sceptical in its implications. Far from it. It is part of a committed
anticatholicism.[12]

There are other episodes in the play which relate to
deception: Almeda's betrayal of Tamburlaine, for instance, or the
governor of Babylon's ironic betrayal of principle. But the centre
of interest shifts again. And it focuses this time on what becomes
the play's principal concern. And that is stoicism.[13]

The dominant discourse was unambiguous in its
condemnation of social rising and in its insistence that wrongdoing
will always be punished. 'All subjects', says the *Homily* 'Of
Obedience':

> are bounden to obey their magistrates, and for no cause
> to resist (or withstand), rebel, or make any sedition
> against them, yea, although they be wicked men. And let
> no man think that he can escape unpunished that
> committeth treason, conspiracy, or rebellion against his
> Sovereign Lord the King, though he commit the same
> never so secretly, either in thought, word, or deed, never
> so privily in his privy chamber by himself, or openly
> communicating and consulting with other. For treason
> will not be hid; treason will out at the length.
>
> (*Two Books of Homilies*, page 113)

And it cites examples from scripture of the punishment visited by
God on the presumptuous, among them Korah, Dathan and Abiram,
and Absalom (page 113). The *Homily* 'Against Disobedience',
issued in 1570 in the wake of the northern rebellion of the previous

year, is if anything more emphatic: 'Such subjects as are
disobedient or rebellious against their princes disobey God, and
procure their own damnation' (*Two Books of Homilies*, page 553).

Marlowe weaves this discourse into the text of both plays,
especially the earlier one. Cosroe asks, 'What means this devilish
shepherd to aspire / With such a giantly presumption?' (II. 6. 1-2).
Bajazeth warns Tamburlaine that 'ambitious pride' shall make him
'fall as low' as himself (IV. 2. 76). And the soldan of Egypt vows
that he will 'rue the day, the hour, / Wherein he wrought such
ignominious wrong / Unto the hallow'd person of a prince' (IV. 3.
38-40). In the later play, the king of Jerusalem warns him that:

> Thy victories are grown so violent
> That shortly heaven, fill'd with the meteors
> Of blood and fire thy tyrannies have made,
> Will pour down blood and fire on thy head,
> Whose scalding drops will pierce thy seething brains,
> And with our bloods, revenge our bloods on thee.
>
> (Part II, IV. 1. 138-43)

And though the calls for vengeance by Orcanes and the kings of
Trebizon and Soria are expressed in secular, humanist terms —
Rhadamanth, Aeacus, Dis (IV. 1. 170-9; IV. 3. 32-42) — what is
being articulated is the dominant ideology.

This prompts one to expect that Tamburlaine will be punished;
that, like Absalom for attempting to displace his king and father
David, he will suffer a 'strange and notable death' ('Of Obedience',
Two Books of Homilies, page 113).[14] The triumphant conclusion to
the earlier play, however, manifestly denies this. And it is at this
juncture that, in relation to the later play, stoicism becomes
important.

In Act II, Scene 4, Zenocrate dies. And the text articulates the
sense of an external, threatening force: 'the malice of the angry
skies' (line 11). In fact, Zenocrate is simply ill. And after the
opening hyperbole of the scene ('Black is the beauty of the brightest

day . . .' [lines 1-37]), Marlowe makes Tamburlaine ask, 'Physicians, will no physic do her good?' (line 38). The question is matter-of-fact; as is the reply: 'My lord . . . / And if she pass this fit, the worst is past' (lines 39-40). Tamburlaine's words to Zenocrate, moreover, though marked by playfulness and concern, are ordinary: 'Tell me, how fares my fair Zenocrate?' (line 41). Zenocrate's reply is a crucial moment in the drama. It is the moment that gives centre and presence to this aspect of the play's multiple discourse. Elsewhere, in both plays, Zenocrate tends to be at once idealised and subordinated. But here she speaks with the full authority of the text:

> I fare, my lord, as other empresses,
> That, when this frail and transitory flesh
> Hath suck'd the measure of that vital air
> That feeds the body with his dated health,
> Wanes with enforc'd and necessary change.
>> (Part II, II. 4. 42-6)

The moment registers a sense of limit which had been refused in the earlier play. But it is an intrinsic, natural limit: a matter of fact. The body has a 'dated health' (line 45). And the limit is universal. Even the most exalted — even Elizabeth herself — wane with 'enforc'd and necessary change' (line 46).

And the appropriate response to this is the stoic one: 'bear and forbear'. Zenocrate dies patiently: 'Let me die, my love; yet, let me die; / With love and patience let your true love die' (lines 66-7). And the text marks her death as exemplary. 'Sweet sons, farewell!', she says:

> In death resemble me,
> And in your lives your father's excellency.
>> (Part II, II. 4. 75-6)

Tamburlaine's response is actually one of impatience. He calls on Techelles to wound the earth, descend with him to hell, and take

revenge on the fates; and on Usumcasane and Theridamas to
shatter the universe with their cannon (lines 96-108). The passage
is marked by a return to hyperbole. And Marlowe signals the
inappropriateness of the response. 'Behold me here, divine
Zenocrate', he makes Tamburlaine declare of himself, '/ Raving,
impatient, desperate and mad' (lines 111-12). And there is a final
advocacy of stoicism through Theridamas: 'Ah, good my lord, be
patient! She is dead, / And all this raging cannot make her live . . . /
Nothing prevails, for she is dead, my lord' (lines 119-24).

Tamburlaine learns the lesson of stoicism. The drama is seen
to act out its own morality. Diegesis is homologous with narrative.
In Act III, Scene 2, after the burning of Larissa, he accepts
Zenocrate's death: 'Sorrow no more, my sweet Casane, now. /
Boys' — to his sons — 'leave to mourn' (lines 44-5). They,
however, continue to mourn. And he responds briskly: 'But now,
my boys, leave off, and list to me' (line 53); and launches
energetically into his speech about the 'rudiments of war' (lines 54-
92) . In reply, Calyphas emerges as weak and pitiful. And
Tamburlaine reacts by cutting his arm. The emblematic nature of
the action is foregrounded by the text. 'Let the burning of Larissa
walls', Tamburlaine proclaims:

> My speech of war, and this my wound you see,
> Teach you, my boys, to bear courageous minds.
>   (Part II, III. 2. 141-3)

And he takes up the struggle with the Turks. The stoic acceptance
of death is followed by the active prosecution of war. The play acts
out Zenocrate's injunction to resemble her in death, and
Tamburlaine's prowess in life.

It is here that the episode of Olympia and Theridamas comes
into play. Olympia appears immediately after Tamburlaine accepts
his wife's death. It is a scene in which Theridamas and Techelles
actively carry forward the war. And Olympia is no more than a
silent presence in it. She first speaks in the following scene, when

she kills her son and Theridamas falls in love with her. Her final appearance, when she deceives Theridamas into killing her, comes just four scenes before Tamburlaine's own death. The episode is carefully placed in relation to — actually, subordinated to — Tamburlaine's development.

Olympia is a representation of stoic resolution. Like Zenocrate, she is idealised at the same time as subordinated. And the killing of her son is endorsed, even though it transgresses the dominant prohibition of murder (Exodus XX. 13).[15] The prohibition is present in the text, and is foregrounded at the moment of the killing: 'Ah sacred Mahomet', she cries, 'if this be sin, / Entreat a pardon of the God of heaven, / And purge my soul before it comes to thee!' (III. 4. 3l-3); but is brushed aside through Techelles:

> 'Twas bravely done, and like a soldier's wife.
> Thou shalt with us to Tamburlaine the Great,
> Who when he hears how resolute thou wert,
> Will match thee with a viceroy or a king.
> (Part II, III. 4. 38-41)

Similarly with her death. The scene opens with her as an emblem of endurance in the face of an external reality she cannot control; and ends with her ingenious escape from it by means of suicide. There is no criticism of her for this, despite the dominant prohibition of self-murder, only praise for her steadfastness. To Theridamas she is one:

> In whom the learned rabbis of this age
> Might find as many wondrous miracles
> As in the theoria of the world!
> (Part II, IV. 2. 84-6)

She is an instructive mystery: a criterion for the audience to judge their own behaviour by as well as Tamburlaine's. She is 'this queen

of chastity' (IV. 2. 96). And he will entomb her 'with all the pomp /
The treasure of [his] kingdom may afford' (IV. 2. 97 to the end).
The advocacy of stoicism in the play is prepared to envisage radical
transgression.

The killing of Olympia's son prefigures Tamburlaine's killing
of Calyphas two scenes later; just as her death prepares the
audience for his. When he first feels ill, his response is one of
defiance: 'Whatsoe'er it be, / Sickness or death can never conquer
me' (V. 1. 219 to the end). And it continues into the play's last
scene. Its unfittingness, however, is signified not only in the
hyperbole of his command to Theridamas: 'haste to the court of
Jove; / Will him to send Apollo hither straight / To cure me, or I'll
fetch him down myself' (V. 3. 61-3); but also in Theridamas' and
Techelles' comments: 'Ah good my lord, leave these impatient
words, / Which add much danger to your malady' (V. 3. 54-5). As
with Zenocrate's death, Marlowe emphasises the naturalness of
Tamburlaine's illness. Its details are firmly rooted in the medical
discourse of the day.[16] And Tamburlaine comes to accept his
mortality. Reluctantly at first: 'Sit still, my gracious lord; this
grief will cease, / And cannot last, it is so violent' . . . 'Not last,
Techelles? No, for I shall die' (V. 3. 64-6). Then more firmly:

> my martial strength is spent;
> In vain I strive and rail against those powers
> That mean t'invest me in a higher throne.
>
> (Part II, V. 3. 119-21)

The lesson of stoicism is relearned. And the homology between
diegesis and narrative in this aspect of the play's meaning is
restored.[17]

As before, stoic acceptance leads to wordly activity. And
Tamburlaine calls for a map, not only to review his career but also to
see what land is left to conquer. The play shifts focus again at this
point. From the start of the scene, Tamburlaine has been referred to
as a king: 'our sovereign' (V. 3. 14); 'your majesty' (V. 3. 78, 98,

102); 'your highness' and 'your royal presence' (V. 3. 110, 111). And the play comes to focus on the question of succession. Elizabeth had been on the throne for nearly thirty years when the play was written. And the contemporary anxiety about who was to succeed her is displaced onto the text.[18] Marlowe, incorporated into the ruling class, is concerned to show an orderly succession. And he does this by altering history. According to Whetstone, Tamburlaine's sons were 'every way far unlike their father' (*English Mirror,* Book I, Chapter 12); whereas Amyras and Celebinus are very much like their father. Calyphas, who is not, is ruthlessly purged from the text: an event not in Whetstone or Perondini. Whetstone, moreover, attributed the decline of Tamburlaine's empire after his death to the 'envy and discord' of his sons (*English Mirror*, Book I, Chapter 12). In the play, Amyras is crowned in public view. And the narrative closes with the succession undisputed and assured.

Marlowe presents the succession in the same naturalistic terms as Tamburlaine's illness. It is a natural inheritance that achieves a kind of immortality. 'Here, lovely boys', he makes Tamburlaine say after surveying the unconquered lands, 'what death forbids my life, / That let your lives command in spite of death' (V. 3. 159-60). And a little later: 'My flesh, divided in your precious shapes, / Shall still retain my spirit, though I die, / And live in all your seeds immortally' (V. 3. 172-4). And he does the same with Tamburlaine's death. Amyras is overcome with grief at its prospect. But Tamburlaine composes the moment with a magisterial pronouncement:

> Let not thy love exceed thine honour, son,
> Nor bar thy mind that magnanimity
> That nobly must admit necessity.
> > (Part II, V. 3. 199-201)

It is, in fact, a key assertion in the play, with its twin concepts of acceptance and natural limit: 'admit necessity' (line 201). And it is endorsed through Theridamas:

> My lord, you must obey his majesty,
> Since fate commands and proud necessity.
>
> (Part II, V. 3. 204-5)

Tamburlaine's death, in short, is presented not as retribution, but as part of natural process; the result, like his wife's death, of 'enforc'd and necessary change'. Marlowe here uses the discourse of history to subvert the dominant morality. For Whetstone recorded how 'in the end this great personage, without disgrace of fortune, after sundry great victories, by the course of nature died, and left behind him two sons' (*English Mirror*, Book I, Chapter 12). And the proper response is acceptance, not grief.

The play concludes with a powerful assertion of imperial ambition. Amyras mounts Tamburlaine's chariot, drawn by captive foreign kings, and is enjoined to 'Bridle the steeled stomachs of those jades' (V. 3. 202-3): the conquered peoples. And there is Tamburlaine's final speech, with its strong sense of imperial destiny in the image of the chariot as the sun and in the authoritative advice given to Amyras. Marlowe draws on humanist discourse here to support an expansionist policy. The imperial chariot is as dangerous as Phaethon's; and must be guided by someone as disciplined as Apollo or Tamburlaine (V. 3. 230-44). The glance at Elizabeth, both admiration and admonition, seems obvious.

The ideology of empire continues unaltered to the end of the play. The ideology of individualism shifts, under the impact of a sense of natural limit, to a radical stoicism.

Chapter Three

The *Jew of Malta*: Policy and Greed

One crucial intertextuality for an understanding of the *Jew of Malta*, which Marlowe most likely wrote in 1589-90, is not with the emergent humanist drama of which *Tamburlaine* is an example, but with the residual drama of mystery play and morality. Barabas is conceived in the mould not of a renaissance hero, but of Herod or the vice: a character like Covetous in William Wager's *Enough Is as Good as a Feast*, written some twenty years before. Barabas is a comic villain; one who 'walk[s] abroad a-nights, / And kill[s] sick people groaning under walls' (II. 3. 172-3). And the play is a tragic farce.[1]

Like Tamburlaine, however, Barabas dominates the play. He provides its centre of interest, and sets in motion most of its action. And the play's attitude towards him is foregrounded right at the outset. He 'favours' — resembles — Machiavelli (Prologue, line 35). For most Elizabethans, machiavellianism was synonymous with deception: with 'policy'.[2] And all Barabas's activities are motivated by it. Some of them have no other motive: the destruction of Lodowick and Mathias, for example. Although the death of Lodowick is prompted by a desire for revenge on Ferneze, there is no reason for the death of Mathias or the desolation of Abigail. They are prompted simply by policy; and amount to motiveless malignity, if ever there was any.

Marlowe enunciates this near the beginning of the episode, when he makes Barabas comment directly to the audience that they will see him have 'more of the serpent than the dove; that is, more knave than fool' (II. 3. 36-7). It is an instance of direct address by Barabas that is characteristic of the play, and which is precisely in the manner of the vice. Once the episode is concluded, moreover, Marlowe sums it up in a soliloquy that he gives to Abigail. The dramatic fiction here is that Abigail is talking to herself, not to the audience. She is thinking aloud. But Marlowe still directs the audience's response in one direction rather than another:

> Hard-hearted father, unkind Barabas!
> Was this the pursuit of thy policy,
> To make me show them favour severally,
> That by my favour they should both be slain?
> Admit thou lov'dst not Lodowick for his sire,
> Yet Don Mathias ne'er offended thee.
> But thou wert set upon extreme revenge,
> Because the Governor dispossess'd thee once,
> And couldst not venge it but upon his son;
> Nor on his son but by Mathias' means;
> Nor on Mathias but by murdering me.
>
> (III. 3. 36-46)

Machiavelli, though, was a political writer. Modern political discourse to an extent stems from him. And political machiavellianism forms an important part of the play. It is not confined, either, to Barabas. At the beginning of the play, the Maltese government owes the Turkish empire money: ten years' tribute. The amount is too much to pay at once. And Calymath grants them a month in which to raise it. Although Ferneze says they will do this by collecting it from the 'inhabitants of Malta' (I. 2. 21), the intention all along has clearly been to collect it from the Jews, and from the Jews alone (I. 2. 69-70). In this, Marlowe is recording historical practice since, from the middle ages, European governments had raised money by special impositions on the Jews. The point to stress, however, is that he does not criticise Ferneze or the knights of Malta for it. And this brings one to another crucial intertextuality. And that is with the common European discourse of antisemitism.[3] Marlowe draws on the discourse as Ferneze and the second knight justify the imposition. When Barabas protests, 'Are strangers with your tribute to be tax'd?', the knight retorts, 'Have strangers leave with us to get their wealth? / Then let them with us contribute'. And when Barabas rejoins, 'How, equally?', Ferneze peremptorily ends the matter. The objection is very deeply repressed by the discourse:

> No, Jew, like infidels;
> For through our sufferance of your hateful lives,
> Who stand accursed in the sight of heaven,
> These taxes and afflictions are befall'n.
>   (I. 2. 60-6)

Nor is the discourse compromised by the pleas for sympathy made by Barabas after his goods are seized (I. 2. 93-158). On the contrary, it is reinforced. This is done partly by direct assertion within the text: by diegesis. Shortly after Barabas has lost everything, the first knight says to him:

> If your first curse fall heavy on thy head,
> And make thee poor and scorn'd of all the world,
> 'Tis not our fault, but thy inherent sin;
>   (I. 2. 106-8)

where the discursive transfer is from Matthew, when the Jews took responsibility for Christ's death: 'His blood be on us, and on our children' (XXVII. 25).[4] And it is done partly by the narrative. Barabas laments his fate to the three Jews. And they respond sympathetically, seeing him as a latter-day Job (I. 2. 159-212). But on their departure, his tone changes. And his lamentation is revealed by Marlowe to have been self-conscious melodrama. 'See the simplicity of these base slaves', he declares:

> Who, for the villains have no wit themselves,
> Think me to be a senseless lump of clay,
> That will with every water wash to dirt!
> No, Barabas is born to better chance,
> And fram'd of finer mould than common men.
>
> 　　　　　　　　(I. 2. 213-18)

Moreover, like the governor of Babylon in the previous play, he turns out to have taken politic precautions against just such an eventuality. In response to Abigail's daughterly indignation, Marlowe gives him these words:

> Be silent, daughter . . .
> 　　　　　　　　think me not all so fond
> As negligently to forgo so much
> Without provision for thyself and me.
> Ten thousand portagues, besides great pearls,
> Rich costly jewels, and stones infinite,
> Fearing the worst of this before it fell,
> I closely hid.
>
> 　　　　　　　　(I. 2. 237, 240-6)[5]

With the arrival of Del Bosco in Act II, Scene 2, however, the Maltese government breaks the treaty with the Turks. Ferneze is persuaded to this by the first knight and by Del Bosco himself. And Marlowe recreates the situation between Sigismund and Orcanes. This time, though, there is no final criticism of the christian ruler. There is some: in lines 28-33, when Del Bosco censures Ferneze for weakness in the face of the Turkish threat ('Will Knights of Malta be in league with Turks . . . '). But the play endorses the breaking of the treaty and the consequent defiance of the infidel. 'Barbarous mis-believing', Ferneze calls the Turks in line 46. Marlowe even rewrites history in order to strengthen the endorsement. The knights surrendered to the Turks at the siege of Rhodes in 1522. They did not fight to the death, as Del Bosco asserts in lines 47-51. And Ferneze's concluding flourish suppresses any irony: 'Honour is bought with blood, and not with gold' (line 56).

This is machiavellian enough. It follows Machiavelli's advice that 'a prudent ruler cannot keep his word, nor should he, when such fidelity would damage him, and when the reasons that made him promise are no longer relevant'.[6] But there is more to the situation than this. Del Bosco advises Ferneze to keep the gold as a prelude to breaking the treaty (II. 2. 39). And Ferneze does this (III. 5. 7-28). Yet the gold is not returned to the Jews, although the occasion for levying it has now passed. It is a further machiavellian twist. And Marlowe totally represses any criticism of Ferneze for it. It is left implicit in the action. And the text is silent about it. Marlowe does not even allow Barabas to object.[7]

Barabas's political machiavellianism appears at the end of the play. And Marlowe's attitude towards it is quite different from that towards Ferneze's. It is one of foregrounded censure: in the manner of the moralities. In Act V, Scene 1, when the conflict between the Maltese and the Turks resurfaces, Barabas betrays the town by leading the Turks in through the sewers. In the next scene, Ferneze and the knights are led in as Calymath's captives. It is a moment corresponding to the Sigismund and Orcanes episode when Sigismund enters defeated: a moment of just punishment for doing wrong. As Calymath says, 'Ferneze, speak; had it not been much better / T'have kept thy promise than be thus surpris'd?' (V. 2. 4-5). On this occasion, however, there is no sense of religious retribution; in fact, little sense of retribution at all. Certainly, Ferneze is not repentant. And repentance is not expected of him by the text. His reply is simply a statement of fact: 'What should I say? We are captives, and must yield' (V. 2. 6). And the play proceeds to remove sympathy from his captor by presenting him as cruel and unforgiving, in contrast to the sympathetic way he was presented at the start of the play. 'Ay, villains', he declares, 'you must yield, and under Turkish yokes / Shall groaning bear the burden of our ire' (V. 2. 7-8). Barabas is then made governor instead of Ferneze. And Marlowe makes his attitude towards him unmistakable. 'Thus hast thou gotten, by thy policy,' he makes Barabas say to himself:

> No simple place, no small authority:
> I now am Governor of Malta; true,
> But Malta hates me, and in hating me
> My life's in danger; and what boots it thee,
> Poor Barabas, to be the Governor,
> Whenas thy life shall be at their command?
> No, Barabas, this must be look'd into;
> And, since by wrong thou got'st authority,
> Maintain it bravely by firm policy.
>
> (V. 2. 27-36)

The key words in these lines are clear: 'policy' (line 27), 'wrong' (line 35), 'firm policy' (line 36); and clearly directive of the audience's response.

Barabas is an opportunist. And he calls in Ferneze, and proposes to free him and destroy the Turks — for a price. Through Barabas, Marlowe explicates the action: 'Thus loving neither, will I live with both, / Making a profit of my policy' (V. 2. 109-10); then draws on antisemitic discourse: 'This is the life we Jews are us'd to lead' (V. 2. 113); and completes the alienation of Barabas from the Elizabethan audience by making him turn directly towards them and, in a characteristic way, openly affront them: 'And reason too, for Christians do the like' (V. 2. 114). Ferneze, of course, turns Barabas's final stratagem back on himself, but not before Marlowe comments on it. It is a typical speech: ironical, but unambiguous in its evaluations; spoken straight to the audience who, while amused by its hilarity, are nonetheless estranged by its shamelessness. 'Why', says Barabas:

> is not this
> A kingly kind of trade, to purchase towns
> By treachery, and sell 'em by deceit?
> Now tell me, worldlings, underneath the sun
> If greater falsehood ever has been done.
>
> (V. 5. 49-53)[8]

Ferneze's betrayal of Barabas is seen quite differently. It is an appropriate response to the 'unhallow'd deeds of Jews' (V. 5. 94). It is 'treachery repaid' (V. 5. 76). Even the massacre of Calymath's soldiers — 'A Jew's courtesy', as Ferneze sardonically calls it (V. 5. 110) — though treacherous when Barabas plans it, becomes no more than justice when its outcome is to place Calymath in Ferneze's hands. 'For he that did by treason work our fall', he says to Calymath, '/ By treason hath deliver'd thee to us' (V. 5. 111-12).

The play actually undergoes a remarkable transformation at the end, parallel to the change at the end of *Tamburlaine*, Part II. Both plays exhibit a trace of the patriotic and religious closure of an earlier drama like *Enough Is as Good as a Feast*.[9] Malta is revealed to be not only a site of imperial struggle between christianity and islam, specifically between Europe and Turkey, but also a site of displacement for England: the beleaguered island. Ferneze and the knights start to figure as the English; in particular, as the English government, of which, however marginally, Marlowe was a part. The Turks start to figure as the Spanish; more widely, as any foreign power that might threaten England. And they are treated humanely, not as if by Jews, but by true christians. As Ferneze says to Calymath of Barabas's stratagem: 'Thus he determin'd to have handled thee, / But I have rather chose to save thy life' (V. 5. 95-6). Nevertheless, they are treated firmly. 'Know therefore', he declares:

> till thy father hath made good
> The ruins done to Malta and to us,

Thou canst not part; for Malta shall be freed,
Or Selim ne'er return to Ottoman.
(V. 5. 113-16)

And the firmness shifts to defiance. Like Walsingham, Ferneze
voices an aggressive policy, registering a new English
confidence after the defeat of the armada. 'Content thee,
Calymath', he continues, 'here thou must stay, / And live in Malta
prisoner':

for come all the world
To rescue thee, so will we guard us now,
As sooner shall they drink the ocean dry,
Than conquer Malta, or endanger us.
(V. 5. 120-4)

And given the systematic repression of criticism of Ferneze, the
play concludes without irony. The dominant discourse is finally
asserted:

So march away; and let due praise be given,
Neither to Fate nor Fortune, but to Heaven.
(V. 5. 125 to the end)[10]

The play, then, constructs a double ideology. What is
acceptable in Ferneze, the representative of English government, is
not acceptable in Barabas, the alien individual.

The play is duplicitous in other ways too. It is set at the Turkish
siege of Malta in 1565. But Marlowe makes little attempt at
historical veracity. The knights never paid tribute to the Turks
who, after the intervention of Spanish troops, simply sailed away.
Nor was there a rich Jew of Malta. And yet, like *Tamburlaine*, the
text claims the authority of history.[11]

There were, however, wealthy Jews in Europe in the sixteenth century, as capital became increasingly important. And the context pressing most closely on the play is the rise of capitalism. Primarily, this was a matter of agriculture. More's maneating sheep are a witness to its early impact.[12] It was also a matter of industry: the remarkable development of coalmining, for example. But its second most important area was trade: the exchange of commodities. And before he is anything, Barabas is a merchant.

Marlowe makes this apparent right at the beginning. The play opens with Barabas compiling his accounts:

> So that of thus much that return was made;
> And of the third part of the Persian ships
> There was the venture summ'd and satisfied.
> As for those Samnites, and the men of Uz,
> That bought my Spanish oils and wines of Greece,
> Here have I purs'd their paltry silverlings.
>   (I. 1. 1-6)

The dramatic fiction here, like that of Abigail's in Act III, Scene 3, is very different from that of the vice. The audience understands itself as overhearing someone actually speaking. Hence the start in mid-sentence. And with the entry of the merchants, there is an abundance of commercial detail which would have been instantly recognised by the predominantly citizen audience: bills of entry, credit, customs dues, transport; the argosy which may not be as seaworthy as it should; the news of its arrival with its fabulous riches ('Persian silks . . . gold, and orient pearl', I. 1. 88); a pragmatic discussion of how it was missed by the other ships; and a dispassionate acceptance of the political connections of trade — it was convoyed by the Spanish as protection against the Turks. Then immediate practicality: disembark and unload its cargo (I. 1. 48-101). The new economy is seen to produce a new subjectivity: an early fetishising of commodity; and a new writing: an emergent naturalism.

Barabas is a merchant capitalist. And, in a crucial ideological turn, Marlowe equates capitalism with machiavellianism. Barabas 'favours' Machiavelli. And his 'money was not got without [his] means' (Prologue, lines 35, 32).[13] He also establishes a further intertextuality crucial to the play's meaning. And that is with the feudal discourse against greed: against capital accumulation. As Matthew puts it, 'Lay not up treasures for yourselves upon the earth . . . But lay up treasures for yourselves in heaven . . . For where your treasure is, there will your heart be also' (VI. 19-21).[14] And, in another crucial ideological turn, Marlowe interweaves this discourse with the discourse of antisemitism. The capitalist is not only a machiavel. He is also a Jew. One can see this in the soliloquy he gives to Barabas as soon as the merchants have left. 'Thus trolls our fortune in by land and sea', he says, ' / And thus are we on every side enrich'd':

> These are the blessings promis'd to the Jews,
> And herein was old Abram's happiness:
> What more may heaven do for earthly man
> Than thus to pour out plenty in their laps,
> Ripping the bowels of the earth for them,
> Making the sea their servant, and the winds
> To drive their substance with successful blasts;
>
> (I. 1. 102-10)

where the ironical inversion of the anticapitalist discourse in lines 106-10 immediately serves to mark Barabas as both different and deviant.

Marlowe recognises the contemporary connection between trade and finance: between mercantile and financial capital. Barabas is both 'a merchant and a money'd man' (I. 2. 54). And, like his audience, he is well aware of the international ramifications of capital by the 1580s. Barabas has dealings with all the great commercial centres of late sixteenth-century Europe: debts and deposits in Florence, Venice, Antwerp, London, Seville, Frankfurt, and Lübeck — even Moscow (IV. 1. 71-4). And yet Marlowe makes Barabas comment a little later in the first scene:

> They say we are a scatter'd nation:
> I cannot tell; but we have scambled up
> More wealth by far than those that brag of faith.
> There's Kirriah Jairim, the great Jew of Greece,
> Obed in Bairseth, Nones in Portugal,
> Myself in Malta, some in Italy,
> Many in France, and wealthy every one.
>
> (I. 1. 120-6)

In fact, European commerce was not dominated by Jews. In England, for example, they had been expelled in 1290; and were not readmitted until 1655. And only a few were living in England at the time of the play.[15] Instead, it was dominated by great European banking families like the Fuggers in Germany. Nor is the list of names historical. They are taken from the old testament; even the place name, Bairseth. And only Nones has some historical reference: to Hector Nunez, the head of the Jewish community in London, and a man almost certainly known to Marlowe's audience. Although a merchant, however, as well as a doctor, he was not a figure typical of late sixteenth-century capitalism. Much more representative was someone like Sir Thomas Gresham, who was a major European figure in the 1550s and 60s. Gresham's father had been a mercer and a lord mayor of London who gained considerably from the sale of monastic land. And his uncle, who taught him business, was a founder of the Russia company. He was appointed king's merchant at Antwerp in 1552, adjusting the exchange rate and raising loans. He became a close friend of Burghley's, influencing economic policy and (like Marlowe) providing foreign intelligence. He built the first English papermills in 1565; and arranged for loans to be raised from London merchants, not foreigners. And in 1566 he built the Royal Exchange in London on the model of the exchange at Antwerp. Characteristically, the text displaces the traditional antipathy towards accumulation from the actual capitalist to the stereotype of the Jew.

In particular, Barabas is a moneylender. In the middle ages, lending money at interest was illegal. But as the economy expanded in the sixteenth century, credit became essential. And it was gradually legalised. By an act of 1545 interest was allowed up to ten per cent. The act was repealed in 1552; but finally reenacted in 1571. Nevertheless, the discursive antipathy towards interest continued. 'Lend, looking for nothing again' are Christ's words in Luke (VI. 35). And the act of 1571 declared that 'all usury being forbidden by the law of God is sin and detestable'.[16] Historically, of course, Jews were moneylenders. But in the sixteenth century, moneylenders were not typically Jews. They were European. Gresham's father, for instance, lent money to Henry VIII's court. And at one time, the emperor Charles V owed the Fuggers two million guldens. Marlowe's text effaces this; and continues its displacement. In his famous self-description in Act II, Scene 3, Barabas recounts his career as a moneylender:

> with extorting, cozening, forfeiting . . .
> I fill'd the gaols with bankrupts in a year,
> And with young orphans planted hospitals,
> And every moon made some or other mad,
> And now and then one hang himself for grief,
> Pinning upon his breast a long great scroll
> How I with interest tormented him.
>
> (II. 3. 189, 191-6)

Later, in his mock confession, the displacement is complete:

> I have been zealous in the Jewish faith,
> Hard-hearted to the poor, a covetous wretch,
> That would for lucre's sake have sold my soul.
> A hundred for a hundred I have ta'en.
>
> (IV. 1. 51-4)

He has charged interest at a hundred per cent.

A decade later, in a rapidly changing culture, Dekker was to legitimate merchant capital in the marriage between Rose, the daughter of Sir Roger Oatley, lord mayor of London, and Lacy, the heir of the earl of Lincoln. Lincoln opposes the marriage: 'Her blood is too too base' (*Shoemaker's Holiday*, Scene 21, line 103). So does Oatley. But it is endorsed by the king, who is the final authority in the drama:

> Lincoln, no more.
> Dost thou not know that love respects no blood,
> Cares not for difference of birth or state?
> The maid is young, well born, fair, virtuous,
> A worthy bride for any gentleman.
>
> (Scene 21, lines 103-7)[17]

The episode enacts the merging of merchant and landed capital, under the aegis of the monarchy, that was a mark of the time. It is a step in the striking transformation of the capitalist from villain to hero which occurred between the sixteenth and eighteenth centuries.[18] Marlowe, writing just a few years before, combines the figure of the vice with the new figure of the machiavel and the old figure of the Jew in order to negotiate, essentially reject, the recent phenomenon of the capitalist. And he does this in the interest of the ruling power. But he does it without alienating capital.

Chapter Four

Edward II: Power and Love

The effacement of the *Jew of Malta* is absent from *Edward II*, which was probably written in 1591. The text is once more grounded on the humanist conviction that truth is to be found in history; and on the most recent authority: Raphael Holinshed's *Chronicles of England, Scotland, and Ireland*, first printed in 1577. Like Holinshed, Marlowe is concerned with the history of the ruling class: with political power; and in particular, with the power of the monarchy. And he both registers and advocates a radical disjunction from the past.[1]

One can see this in his representation of the feudal nobility under Edward. They are proud, unruly, and ambitious. 'Base leaden earls that glory in your birth', says Gaveston to them with a contempt endorsed by the text, '/ Go sit at home and eat your tenants' beef' (II. 2. 74-5). As a class, they are unproductive. And their objection to Gaveston is as much to his low birth as to his pernicious effect on the king. Mortimer's angry disdain for him early in the play reveals their disorderly self-interest:

> Were all the earls and barons of my mind,
> We'll hale him from the bosom of the King,
> And at the court gate hang the peasant up,

Who, swoln with venom of ambitious pride,
Will be the ruin of the realm and us.
                    (I. 2. 28-32)

But its full extent is seen at Gaveston's reunion with the king
in Act II, Scene 2. It is a moment of archetypal disorder in the
text. The focus of the barons' emotion is again Gaveston. And
they greet him sarcastically (lines 64-8). Prompted by Edward,
Gaveston replies with contempt (lines 74-5); then adds:

Come not here to scoff at Gaveston,
Whose mounting thoughts did never creep so low,
As to bestow a look on such as you.
                    (II. 2. 76-8).

To which Lancaster retorts, 'Yet I disdain not to do this for you';
and draws his sword (line 79). To produce a weapon in the
presence of the monarch was a serious offence in Elizabeth's day.
In theory at least, it was punishable by death. And there is a
moment of farce as Edward panics. 'Treason, treason!', he shouts;
adding foolishly: 'Where's the traitor?' (line 80). Pembroke
responds coolly and mischievously: 'Here, here!', pointing to
Gaveston (line 81). At which Edward panics further, this time
pathetically: 'Convey hence Gaveston; they'll murder him' (line
82). The action here has great pace. It is highly interactive
between characters. And the language is strongly colloquial. As
an enactment of a specific kind of social chaos, the writing is
superb. Gaveston is firmer than Edward; and turns defiantly to
Lancaster: 'The life of thee shall salve this foul disgrace' (line 83).
But Mortimer compounds the barons' lawlessness by advancing on
him: 'Villain, thy life, unless I miss mine aim'. And he actually
stabs him (line 84).

At this point, Isabella intervenes. It is a decisive, authoritative
intervention that has been lacking in the scene; and which,
according to the dominant discourse, should be coming from the

monarch. Given the hierarchisation of gender, it certainly should
not be coming from his wife. She addresses Mortimer directly and
openly: 'furious Mortimer, what hast thou done?' (line 85). But he
is unrepentant, truculent: 'No more than I would answer were he
slain' (line 86).

  With Gaveston offstage, Edward attempts to assert his authority.
'Yes', he counters, 'more than thou canst answer, though he live' (line
87). Then to both Mortimer and Lancaster: 'Dear shall you both aby
this riotous deed. / Out of my presence! Come not near the court'
(lines 88-9). But the farce recurs. 'I'll not be barr'd the court for
Gaveston', says Mortimer (line 90). And with greater recalcitrance,
Lancaster: 'We'll hale him by the ears unto the block' (line 91).
Edward threatens in reply: 'Look to your own heads; his is sure
enough' (line 92). At which Warwick butts in with a more serious
threat: 'Look to your own crown, if you back him thus' (line 93).
For this, Kent reproves him. But there is then a moment of pure
absurdity, stemming from the weakness as monarch characteristic of
Edward in the earlier part of the play. 'Nay', he complains petulantly
— perhaps to the audience — 'all of them conspire to cross me thus'
(line 95). Followed by an unconvinced, and unconvincing, assertion
of power: 'But if I live', he says uncertainly, 'I'll tread upon their
heads / That think with high looks thus to tread me down' (lines 96-
7). And there is a culminating absurdity when he turns to Kent, and
himself — not the barons — leaves the stage. 'Come Edmund', he
cries, 'let's away and levy men; / 'Tis war that must abate these
barons' pride' (lines 98-9). The world has been turned upside down.
And while the responsibility for this is seen to lie ultimately with the
monarch, its source is represented as lying with the nobility. The
play, in other words, is antifeudal; just as, in its displaced way, the
Jew of Malta was anticapitalist.[2]

Gaveston, by contrast, is not a nobleman. The play is actually
unspecific about Gaveston's social position. But his humble
origins, on the borderline of the gentry, are emphasised by the text,

mainly through the comments of the barons. As Mortimer says at another moment of chronic disorder — his banishment — 'Thou villain, wherefore talkst thou of a king, / That hardly art a gentleman by birth?' (I. 4. 28-9). And the barons characteristically refer to him in terms that are feudal or socially dismissive, much as Tamburlaine was referred to earlier, but more intensively: 'villain', 'peasant', 'vassal', 'base', 'obscure', 'groom'.[3] In fact, Marlowe is altering history here. The discursive transfer is interrupted. Holinshed refers to Gaveston as an 'esquire of Gascogne', the son of a French knight (*Chronicles*, II, 539). And Marlowe turns him into a typically Marlovian figure: the person who, like Marlowe himself, was born low but has risen high.

Baldock is another such figure, and one closer to Marlowe's own case. When he is introduced to Edward, the king asks him, 'Tell me, where wast thou born? What is thine arms?': his coat of arms (II. 2. 241). To which he replies:

> My name is Baldock, and my gentry
> I fetch'd from Oxford, not from heraldry.
> (II. 2. 242-3)

Like Marlowe's, his status as a gentleman derives not from inheritance, but from education. Again, history is being altered. Robert Baldock was lord chancellor between 1323 and 1326, and not a scholar. And Edward's response is important:

> The fitter art thou, Baldock, for my turn;
> Wait on me, and I'll see thou shalt not want.
> (II. 2. 244-5)

Similarly, when Mortimer rebukes Gaveston with his low birth, Edward retorts: 'Were he a peasant' — with the full feudal force of the word —

> being my minion,
> I'll make the proudest of you stoop to him.
> (I. 4. 30-1)

Even Spencer, who was historically one of the barons, is subtly separated from them in the text, and socially downgraded. Their herald refers to him as a 'pernicious upstart' (III. 2. 165). And the king is advised to:

> cherish virtue and nobility,
> And have old servitors in high esteem,
> And shake off smooth dissembling flatterers.
> (III. 2. 167-9)

The play registers the radical decline of feudalism by the 1590s; and the radical difference between Tudor and feudal policy. The Tudors recruited from the gentry or below, and recruited for ability not birth. Hence the substance of the barons' complaint. It was a policy designed to marginalise the feudal nobility and create a new ruling class dependent on the crown. The Bacons, Cavendishes, Cecils, Russells, and Seymours were all creations of the Tudors. One of the most conspicuous examples was Thomas Wolsey. Born about 1475, he was the son of an Ipswich butcher. Educated at Oxford, he followed a brilliant career in the church, and became lord chancellor in 1515. For the next fourteen years, until his fall from royal favour, he was the most powerful person in England after Henry VIII himself. In Elizabeth's reign there is Thomas Egerton, whom Donne worked for in the 1590s. The illegitimate son of a Cheshire squire, he too was educated at Oxford; went on to the Inns of Court; and followed a career in the law. In 1581 Elizabeth appointed him solicitor general. And he took a leading part in the prosecution of Mary, queen of Scots. In 1596 she appointed him lord keeper. And he was made lord chancellor by James on his accession.

Marlowe, himself a product of this policy, endorses it in *Edward II*, as he does in *Tamburlaine*, especially Part I. But there is a shift in discourse between the two plays parallel to the rejection of economic individualism, however disguised, in Barabas. In the earlier work, the commitment to social mobility is absolute, open-ended: 'Nature . . . / Doth teach us all' — without exception — 'to have aspiring minds' (Part I, II. 7. 18, 20). And the ambition is specifically political. The drama asserts, quite extraordinarily for its age, that the struggle for personal power is natural. Most extraordinary of all, it asserts that the ambitious overthrow of monarchy is normal; indeed, desirable. We should never rest 'until we reach the ripest fruit of all . . . / The sweet fruition of an earthly crown' (Part I, II. 7. 27-9). In *Edward II* the recruitment of Baldock, and the elevation of Gaveston and Spencer, are endorsed. As Theridamas says in the earlier play, 'he is gross and like the massy earth / That moves not upwards' (Part I, II. 7. 31-2). And this, despite the cynicism and hypocrisy of Spencer and Baldock, in what amounts to a disruptive moment of anticourt and antipuritan satire (II. 1. 31-51). But the attitude to Mortimer is very different.

At the beginning of the play, Mortimer is little more than one of the barons, who are led by Lancaster and Warwick. But after their execution in Act III, Scene 3, the barons as a class disappear from the text. And Mortimer starts his solitary rise to power. Immediately, his words are those of *Tamburlaine*. His defiance of Edward has the accents and the key terms — 'virtue', 'aspires' — of the earlier work. 'What, Mortimer!', he says as he is taken off to the Tower:

> Can ragged stony walls
> Immure thy virtue that aspires to heaven?
> No Edward, England's scourge, it may not be;
> Mortimer's hope surmounts his fortune far.
> (III. 3. 71-4)

And his words to Gurney after his ascendancy has been achieved rewrite the famous lines of Tamburlaine to Theridamas: 'I hold the Fates bound fast in iron chains, / And with my hand turn Fortune's wheel about' (Part I, I. 2. 174-5). Gurney is exhorted to make the life of Edward a misery, 'as', says Mortimer to him:

> thou intend'st to rise by Mortimer,
> Who now makes Fortune's wheel turn as he please.
> (V. 2. 52-3)

The high point of Mortimer's rise is reached just before the king's murder. And it is expressed in one of the outstanding speeches of the play: a soliloquy that extends the naturalism emergent in the *Jew of Malta* further in the direction of interiority, and which is anticipated in such a speech of Tamburlaine's as his meditation on beauty and manliness — his apostrophe to Zenocrate near the end of Part I:

> The Prince I rule, the Queen do I command,
> And with a lowly congé to the ground
> The proudest lords salute me as I pass.
> I seal, I cancel, I do what I will;
> Fear'd am I more than lov'd: let me be fear'd,
> And when I frown, make all the court look pale.
> I view the Prince with Aristarchus' eyes,
> Whose looks were as a breeching to a boy.
> They thrust upon me the Protectorship,
> And sue to me for that that I desire:
> While at the council-table, grave enough
> And not unlike a bashful puritan,
> First I complain of imbecility,
> Saying it is *onus quam gravissimum*,
> Till being interrupted by my friends,
> *Suscepi* that *provinciam*, as they term it;
> And, to conclude, I am Protector now.

Now all is sure: the Queen and Mortimer
Shall rule the realm, the King; and none rule us.
Mine enemies will I plague, my friends advance,
And what I list command, who dare control?
Maior sum quam cui possit fortuna nocere.
                                        (V. 4. 48-69)

The speech, however, does not create the sense of assured
achievement and ensuing peace that is created at the high point of
Tamburlaine's rise (Part I, V. 1. 504 to the end). Instead, there is an
ironical sense of tragic villainy. Mortimer is represented as having
replaced the barons as the principal source of disorder in the play.
Unfettered individualism has replaced feudal intransigence. Once
more, the subject rules the ruler: 'the Queen and Mortimer / Shall
rule the realm, the King; and none rule us' (lines 65-6). And
though the agency is new, the world is again turned upside down.
    The irony of the speech stems fundamentally from the
character's misconception of his position; a position that the text
privileges the audience to recognise: 'Maior sum quam cui possit
fortuna nocere' (line 69), 'I am greater than anyone that fortune
could harm'. Like Tamburlaine before the death of Zenocrate, he
claims to transcend all external limit; in particular, to be above
every restraint upon his political will: 'What I list command, who
darc control?' (line 68). In a sense, though, his downfall is already
present in the text. In the first place, it was part of the familiar
Elizabethan narrative of feudal history. And in the second, the
intertextuality with Ovid brings it ineluctably into the drama.
Niobe's words, which Marlowe makes Mortimer quote here, come
when she claims to be superior to the goddess Latona and, as a
result, provokes her own destruction: transformation into a pillar
of weeping stone (*Metamorphoses*, VI. 195). Niobe was a classic
instance of pride that was justly punished. And the intertextuality
inevitably brings the whole dominant ideology to bear on the
speech. The subject position which Marlowe constructs for the
audience is one of traditional disapprobation.[4]

The actual downfall takes place in the brief, final scene of the play: in Mortimer's last speech. It is not, strictly speaking, a soliloquy. The stage is full. And the occasion is a highly public one: the dispensation of royal justice. Part of it, too, is spoken to Isabella. But the effect at the beginning is one of alienated interiority:

> Base Fortune, now I see, that in thy wheel
> There is a point, to which when men aspire,
> They tumble headlong down; that point I touch'd,
> And seeing there was no place to mount up higher,
> Why should I grieve at my declining fall?
> Farewell, fair Queen, weep not for Mortimer,
> That scorns the world, and as a traveller
> Goes to discover countries yet unknown.
>
> (V. 6. 59-66)

It is a marvellous moment. The tragic defiance has a special poignancy; and one that was to echo throughout Elizabethan and Jacobean tragedy. But Marlowe is very deliberate in his use of the wheel of fortune, and of the crucial term 'aspire' (line 60). In *Tamburlaine*, they had been used with revolutionary significance. Here they are used to situate the growing individualism of the 1580s and 90s, registered textually in a developing interiority and stemming ultimately from the new economy, within a dominant frame of reference. Mortimer is represented as proud; as having presumed to rise too far; and as justly — even divinely — punished. The discursive transfer from Elizabethan history here is direct. Holinshed refers to Mortimer's 'pride and high presumption'. And he is drawn and hanged at Tyburn (*Chronicles*, II, 597, 598-9). In the play, young Edward calls on God to exact retribution from him:

> So may his limbs be torn, as is this paper:
> Hear me, immortal Jove, and grant it too.
>
> (V. 1. 142-3)

And in the very last moment, his head is produced on stage and placed on Edward's hearse by the new king (V. 6. 93 to the end). The tension implicit in *Tamburlaine* between individualism and monarchy, and provisionally contained within the text, becomes an explicit contradication in *Edward II*. Faced by monarchy, the commitment to open-ended individualism is closed down.

The dominant ideology is reproduced in the drama in another way: in its advocacy of strong monarchy and a unified state. As Marlowe makes Edward say, 'Two kings in England cannot reign at once' (V. 1. 58). Strong rule, however, is something that Edward is unable to achieve; at least, consistently. And his weakness is brought out at various moments. But it is emphasised by Marlowe later in Act II, Scene 2, when Mortimer and Lancaster speak their mind frankly to him (lines 153-98). Given the hierarchical assumptions of the time, in particular that of the preeminence of the ruler, it is an occasion of profound humiliation for him. The accusations are, nevertheless, endorsed: self-indulgence, favouritism, mismanagement of revenues, overtaxation, military weakness, loss of prestige at home and abroad. It is a catalogue of archetypal errors. Marlowe intensifies the historical narrative here; and adds to it. And its specificity is that of the 1590s. Although there was war with Ireland in Edward's reign, for example, it was not central to it. Whereas it was central to Elizabeth's. And 'the wild O'Neill, with swarms of Irish kerns' (line 162) was a source of anxiety to her, but not to Edward. In fact, three years after the play, Hugh O'Neill was to embark on a campaign of Irish resistance that was to trouble the English government throughout the 1590s. Similarly, current concern about commercial rivalry with Denmark is displaced onto the text in Mortimer's accusation that 'the haughty Dane commands the narrow seas, / While in the harbour ride thy ships unrigg'd' (lines 167-8): something quite absent from Holinshed.

It would be a mistake, however, to see Edward as simply a weak monarch; and to see the play as simply presenting an example to be eschewed: exorcising a fear. Towards the end of Act III, Marlowe shows Edward to be capable of decisive action. He defeats the barons and executes their leaders. And the event functions as a renewal of monarchy within the play. 'Edward this day', Marlowe gets him to declare, 'hath crown'd him king anew' (III. 3. 76). Though the old irresponsibility lingers. Three scenes later, when we next see him, he is with the two Spencers. And though his first words are acceptably patriotic: 'Thus after many threats of wrathful war, / Triumpheth England's Edward' (IV. 3. 1-2), he adds: 'with his friends' (IV. 3. 2); and then voices a totally unacceptable sentiment: 'And triumph Edward with his friends uncontroll'd' (IV. 3. 3). The prospect is of a return to the debilitating favouritism that prevailed while Gaveston was alive.

More importantly, there is a marked shift in attitude towards Edward after his defeat by Mortimer and Isabella in Act IV, Scene 5. The event marks a real change in the drama.[5] Formally, it becomes much slower: an effect of the lengthening and centralising of Edward's speeches. Affectively, it generates sympathy for Edward by creating a sense of pity towards him. Marlowe situates the audience for this through the Abbot early on. 'My heart with pity earns' — grieves — 'to see this sight', he says of him (IV. 6. 70). But the pity is less for Edward as a man than it is for Edward as a king. Discursively, Marlowe induces a sense of pathos at the decline of a ruler in order to elevate the notion of kingship. And again the audience is situated for this through the Abbot: 'A king to bear these words and proud commands!' (IV. 6. 71). Marlowe, in short, reinforces the absolutist turn of the dominant ideology. And he does this by accentuating monarchy rather than the monarch: the institution rather than the individual. It is something apparent in practically every speech Edward utters in the final phase of the play. Indeed, after his capture, Marlowe explicitly differentiates the subject from the monarch, and emphasises the otherness of rule. 'The griefs of private men', he makes Edward assert:

> are soon allay'd,
> But not of kings: the forest deer being struck
> Runs to an herb that closeth up the wounds,
> But when the imperial lion's flesh is gor'd
> He rends and tears it with his wrathful paw,
> And highly scorning that the lowly earth
> Should drink his blood, mounts up into the air:
> And so it fares with me.
>
> (V. 1. 8-15)

It is with this emphasis that Marlowe extends the play's historical intertextuality from Holinshed to John Stow's *Chronicles of England*, first published in 1580. The episode of Edward's forcible shaving in puddle water is a moment of further humiliation for him that looks forward to the final humiliation of his murder two scenes later. But, in fact, Marlowe lessens the pathos of Stow's narrative and the humanising of monarchy that it entailed. Edward refused cold water. 'Would they nould they', he said, 'he would have warm water for his beard; and, to the end that he might keep his promise, he began to weep, and to shed tears plentifully'. It is the climax of the narrative; and not only in Stow.[6] But Marlowe omits it. Instead, he stresses the violation of monarchical sanctity. Turning away from Matrevis and Gurney, and perhaps facing the audience, Edward exclaims:

> Immortal powers, that knows the painful cares
> That waits upon my poor distressed soul,
> O level all your looks upon these daring men,
> That wrongs their liege and sovereign, England's king.
>
> (V. 3. 37-40)[7]

The play concludes with a movement parallel to that at the end of *Tamburlaine*, Part II: with the succession assured, the state unified, and monarchical power forcefully affirmed. Edward III, who is viewed sympathetically throughout, is crowned on stage in

Act V, Scene 4. But he does not confront Mortimer until after his
father's death. When he does, there is a sense of strong monarchy
at last. 'Traitor', he says directly to him, 'in me my loving father
speaks, / And plainly saith, 'twas thou that murd'redst him' (V. 6.
41-2). He is supported by his nobles. 'Fear not, my lord, know that
you are a king', the first lord prompts him (V. 6. 24). They are
anonymous. The feudal baron has been replaced by the court
functionary. And the dispensation of justice is open and impartial.
There is no favouritism towards Isabella. 'Mother . . .', Edward
addresses her, 'If you be guilty, though I be your son, / Think not to
find me slack or pitiful' (V. 6. 78, 81-2). Although he is shown to
possess common human feelings which — rightly — he
suppresses. 'Away with her', he tells the lords, 'her words enforce
these tears, / And I shall pity her if she speak again' (V. 6. 85-6).
The difference between him and his father is clearly presented as a
pregnant one.

By the close of the play, however, there is no criticism of
Edward. His suffering, his religious death, and the filial devotion
of his son, all function to absolve him from blame. Rather,
opprobrium is directed towards Mortimer: the representation of
unbridled self-assertion that threatens monarchy. In a gesture that
rewrites the conclusion of the first part of *Tamburlaine*, the young
king puts on funeral robes: inaugurating a new order. And placing
Mortimer's head on his father's hearse as a sign of Mortimer's
submission and defeat, he completes the final tableau:

> Sweet father here, unto thy murder'd ghost,
> I offer up this wicked traitor's head;
> And let these tears distilling from mine eyes
> Be witness of my grief and innocency.
>
> (V. 6. 99 to the end)

In the historical mythology of the time, the reign of Edward III was
one of archetypal greatness; just as that of his father was one of
archetypal weakness. Marlowe here both draws on and reproduces

this duality; and shares with the audience the proleptic knowledge that the events which will follow the conclusion of the drama will form a moment of high achievement in English history. Rejecting feudal particularism, and uncomfortable with capitalist self-interest, Marlowe chooses to occupy the only other terrain open to his generation: that of royal absolutism.[8]

The play presents no disjunction between the private and the public. Mortimer achieves the power he does through his relationship with Isabella; a relationship that Marlowe actually handles very subtly. And Edward is the weak king he is because of his love for Gaveston; later, because of his love for Spencer. And it is here that the play takes on a specifically Marlovian identity. For the love between Edward and Gaveston is sexual.[9]

Holinshed suppresses this. Edward, he says:

> gave himself to wantonness, passing his time in voluptuous pleasure, and riotous excess: and to help them forward in that kind of life, the foresaid Piers, who (as it may be thought, he had sworn to make the king to forget himself, and the state, to the which he was called) furnished his court with companies of jesters, ruffians, flattering parasites, musicians, and other vile and naughty ribalds, that the king might spend both days and nights in jesting, playing, blanketing, and in such other filthy and dishonourable exercises.
>
> (*Chronicles*, II, 547)

Whereas Marlowe, in the early part of the play, foregrounds it; when, for example, Gaveston enters reading Edward's letter:

> 'My father is deceas'd, come Gaveston,
> And share the kingdom with thy dearest friend.'
> Ah, words that make me surfeit with delight!

> What greater bliss can hap to Gaveston
> Than live and be the favourite of a king?
> Sweet prince I come; these, these thy amorous lines
> Might have enforc'd me to have swum from France,
> And like Leander, gasp'd upon the sand,
> So thou wouldst smile and take me in thy arms.
>
> (I. 1. 1-9)

The physicality of the relationship is made manifest here right at
the beginning of the play: with Gaveston as Leander and Edward,
by implication, the female Hero; and in the sexually-charged
language — 'surfeit', 'bliss', 'amorous', 'gasp'd' (lines 3, 4, 6, and 8).
And it is rendered explicit a little later when Gaveston refers to
Edward as 'him I hold so dear, / The King, upon whose bosom let
me die' (I. 1. 13-14), where Marlowe shares with the audience the
common Elizabethan association of death and orgasm.

In another major moment, Marlowe accentuates the eroticism
of the relationship. It is a rewriting of Holinshed that transforms
the intertext. And again the words are given to Gaveston:

> I must have wanton poets, pleasant wits,
> Musicians, that with touching of a string
> May draw the pliant King which way I please;
> Music and poetry is his delight:
> Therefore I'll have Italian masques by night,
> Sweet speeches, comedies, and pleasing shows;
> And in the day, when he shall walk abroad,
> Like sylvan nymphs my pages shall be clad;
> My men like satyrs grazing on the lawns
> Shall with their goat-feet dance an antic hay;
> Sometime a lovely boy in Dian's shape,
> With hair that gilds the water as it glides,
> Crownets of pearl about his naked arms,
> And in his sportful hands an olive tree
> To hide those parts which men delight to see,

Shall bathe him in a spring; and there hard by,
One like Actaeon peeping through the grove,
Shall by the angry goddess be transform'd,
And running in the likeness of an hart,
By yelping hounds pull'd down, and seem to die.

(I. 1. 50-69)

Although an extraordinary transformation, there is nevertheless a discursive continuity between the two texts. Gaveston, at this initial point of the drama, shows traces of the vice. Alienating the citizen audience: 'The sight of London to my exil'd eyes / Is as Elysium to a new-come soul'; then adding, 'Not that I love the city or the men' (I. 1. 10-12). And misleading the protagonist: he will 'draw the pliant King' which way he pleases (I. 1. 52). In Holinshed, 'he had sworn to make the king to forget himself, and the state, to the which he was called'. And yet the point to emphasise is that there is also a discursive discontinuity. Although Gaveston is represented as manipulating homosexual desire, this does not extend to a rejection of homosexual desire itself; any more than Gaveston's opportunism compromises the commitment to recruitment by ability.

The dominant discourse saw homosexuality as wrong; one among many deviations from the exclusive heterosexual union of marriage. Quoting St Paul (1 Corinthians VI. 9-10), the *Homily* 'Against Whoredom and Uncleanness' warned that 'neither whoremongers . . . nor adulterers, nor softlings, nor sodomites . . . shall inherit the kingdom of God' (*Two Books of Homilies*, page 131); while Leviticus is quite explicit: 'The man . . . that lieth with the male, as one lieth with a woman, they have both committed abomination: they shall die the death' (XX. 13). And in 1563 parliament revived earlier legislation to make the 'detestable and abominable vice of buggery' punishable by death.[10] Marlowe cuts right across this morality. The relationship between Edward and Gaveston is seen to be injurious. But it is injurious to the state. Edward puts his personal interest before the interest of the realm; something which the virgin queen was conspicuous in not doing. He is even prepared to fracture the state. 'Make several kingdoms of this monarchy', he tells the barons:

> And share it equally amongst you all —
> So I may have some nook or corner left
> To frolic with my dearest Gaveston.
>   (I. 4. 70-3)

And yet the relationship is presented as humanly valid; as valid as any relationship in the play.

Marlowe achieves this partly by a use of myth that both validates and celebrates the relationship. After Gaveston's return from France, he makes Edward embrace him and compare his feelings to those of a mythic instance of homosexual loss: 'Not Hylas was more mourn'd of Hercules / Than thou hast been of me since thy exile' (I. 1. 139-44). And three scenes later, drawing on classical history as well as myth, he actively promotes the idea that homosexual love is normal. He does this through the authoritative figure of Mortimer Senior. Since Edward 'so dotes on Gaveston, / Let him without controlment have his will':

> The mightiest kings have had their minions:
> Great Alexander lov'd Hephaestion;
> The conquering Hercules for Hylas wept;
> And for Patroclus stern Achilles droop'd:
> And not kings only, but the wisest men:
> The Roman Tully lov'd Octavius;
> Great Socrates, wild Alcibiades.
>   (I. 4. 388-96)

Marlowe mythologises history here. There was no close relationship between Cicero and Octavian. Nevertheless, the argument continues, as Edward is young, he should be free to 'enjoy that vain light-headed earl, / For riper years will wean him from such toys' (I. 4. 399-400). His fault is not homosexuality, but the giddiness of youth. And the text endorses this when Mortimer, Edward's most implacable enemy in the play, accepts his uncle's words: 'His wanton humour grieves not me' (I. 4. 401). What irks him is the threat not to sexual, but to social, difference:

> this I scorn, that one so basely born
> Should by his sovereign's favour grow so pert . . .
> I will not yield to any such upstart.
>   (I. 4. 402-3, 422)[11]

The commitment to absolutism, itself a departure from traditional notions of limited monarchy, is complemented by a radical homosexuality.[12]

Chapter Five

Doctor Faustus: Science and Religion

Between *Edward II* and *Doctor Faustus*, Marlowe probably wrote the *Massacre at Paris* in 1592. The play, which seems to be a memorial reconstruction, is an ambitious project. It focuses on the history of the French ruling class between the marriage of Henry Bourbon to Margaret Valois in 1572 and Henry's accession to the throne in 1589. Its concern, however, is less with political power than with ideological struggle.

From a different perspective, it is not difficult to see why Marlowe was attracted to the narrative. It contained figures already present in Marlowe's writing and which were clearly significant to him. There was a weak monarch in Charles IX; a ruthless, dominating mother in Catherine de Medici; an ambitious individualist in Guise; a homosexual king and his lovers in Henry III and Maugiron and Joyeuse; a low-born scholar who had risen high — the Marlowe figure itself — in Ramus; and a messianic hero in Henry IV. But what the drama centres on is the contemporary conflict between protestantism and catholicism.

The play is marked by a profound commitment to a nationalist and militant protestantism; a commitment at once anticatholic, antispanish, and antipapal. It makes explicit what is elsewhere implicit or incidental in Marlowe. The commitment is voiced by the prospective Henry IV as he prepares for war in Scene XVI: a representation of events that led to the famous victory of Coultras in 1587, a victory the drama celebrates in Scene XVIII. 'We undertake to manage these our wars', he declares:

> Against the proud disturbers of the faith,
> I mean the Guise, the Pope, and King of Spain;
> (XVI. 2-4)

where Marlowe focuses attention on the three principal protagonists in the enterprise of England: the attempt to depose Elizabeth and restore catholicism that had recently been defeated in the armada.

The play, moreover, foregrounds its parallel between Henry IV and Elizabeth: both major supporters of the protestant cause at the time it was written. Near its conclusion, Henry III turns on his deathbed to Bourbon. It is a moment that takes place in the presence of the English agent; very likely a representation of Walsingham, whose policies the play inscribes, and who stands on stage as a silent and endorsing witness throughout its concluding phase. Despite his homosexuality, Henry III has an ultimate authority as monarch within the play's discourse. 'Navarre, give me thy hand', he says:

>   I here do swear
> To ruinate that wicked Church of Rome,
> That hatcheth up such bloody practices

— his stabbing by the dominican friar, Clément —

> And here protest eternal love to thee,
> And to the Queen of England specially,
> Whom God hath bless'd for hating papistry.
> (XXV. 65-70)

The play ends with an affirmation of the current protestant endeavour in France under Henry IV; and, by displacement, advocates a similar endeavour in England under Elizabeth. The last words of the assassinated Henry III reinforce the connection between the two monarchies:

> I die, Navarre . . .
> Salute the Queen of England in my name,
> And tell her, Henry dies her faithful friend.
> (XXV. 104-6)

And the new king closes the drama. He addresses both the French court and the London audience. 'Come, lords', he orders, 'take up the body of the King, / That we may see it honourably interr'd' (XXV. 107-8). And then, facing the characteristically protestant spectators, 'I vow', he asserts:

> for to revenge his death
> As Rome, and all those popish prelates there,
> Shall curse the time that e'er Navarre was king,
> And rul'd in France by Henry's fatal death.
> (XXV. 109 to the end)[1]

Like the *Massacre at Paris*, *Doctor Faustus* derives from contemporary, or near-contemporary, history. It focuses, however, not on the experience of the ruling class but, as in *Tamburlaine* and the *Jew of Malta* in their differently displaced ways, on that of Marlowe's own class and the class of the majority of his audience: the rising bourgeoisie.

George Helmstetter was probably born in 1466-7 in Helmstadt near Heidelberg. Registered as a student at Heidelberg university in 1483, he took his BA in 1484 and his MA three years later. After apparently teaching at the university for the next two years, he left to become an itinerant scholar, travelling throughout

Germany. By 1507 he had given himself a Latin name in the humanist way: Georgius Sabellicus Faustus junior; and described himself as 'chief of necromancers, astrologer, the second magus, palmist, diviner by earth, diviner by fire, second in the art of divination by water'.[2] He lived at least into his late sixties, one of his last commissions being to prepare a prediction in 1534 for the German explorer Philip von Hutten's expedition to Venezuela. He seems to have died some time before 1539.[3]

Faustus published nothing. And he seems to have been something of a flamboyant character. But what needs to be stressed is that he was not an unrepresentative figure. More prominent, though not essentially different, was his younger contemporary, Mikolaj Kopernik: Nicolaus Copernicus. Nothing is known of Faustus's social origins. But Copernicus was born in 1473 in Torun, Poland, into the urban middle class. He was the son of a merchant. Brought up by his uncle, the prince-bishop of Ermland, he went in 1491 to the university of Cracow, where his studies seem to have included mathematics and astronomy; and spent the next fifteen years in study and travel: to Bologna, where he read law and took an MA; to Rome, where he taught mathematics; to Padua, where he completed his legal studies and learned Greek; to Ferrara, where he took a doctorate in canon law; and back to Padua, to study medicine. He had been made a canon of Frauenburg cathedral in his absence. And in 1506 he returned to Ermland where, in the humanist fashion, he spent the rest of his life in civil and ecclesiastical affairs; among other things, practising as a doctor. In 1543, the year of his death, he finally published a full account of his heliocentric theory, *On the Revolutions of the Heavenly Spheres*; a text he had worked on for some three decades, and which was to prove a watershed in the development of scientific discourse. The historical movement, then, that the play is initially a response to is the rise of science.[4]

The history of Faustus was mythologised, and Faustus himself demonised, as early as the 1530s, especially by Luther.[5] But the account of his life printed in Germany in 1587 nevertheless claimed historicity for its narrative; as did its translation into English, *The History of the Damnable Life and Deserved Death of Doctor John Faustus*, which was published in 1592, and formed Marlowe's principal intertext. It is a historicity, and a consequent authority as truth, also claimed by Marlowe's play.[6]

Like Faustus and Copernicus, Marlowe's protagonist is a renaissance scientist: a universal inquirer, seeking, in particular, natural knowledge.[7] The focus of the rise of science in the sixteenth century was astronomy. One only has to think of the main figures involved: Copernicus himself, Kepler, Galileo. And the science of *Doctor Faustus* characteristically centres on the heavens. There is the voyage of space exploration, for example, recounted by the chorus before Act III:

> Learned Faustus,
> To find the secrets of astronomy
> Graven in the book of Jove's high firmament,
> Did mount him up to scale Olympus top,
> Where sitting in a chariot burning bright,
> Drawn by the strength of yoked dragons' necks,
> He views the clouds, the planets, and the stars,
> The tropics, zones, and quarters of the sky,
> From the bright circle of the horned moon,
> Even to the height of *Primum Mobile*.
> And whirling round with this circumference,
> Within the concave compass of the pole,
> From east to west his dragons swiftly glide,
> And in eight days did bring him home again.
> (Chorus I, lines 1-14)

Marlowe probably wrote the play in 1592-3, at a crucial moment in the acceptance of the heliocentric theory. The work of Dee; of John Feild; of Robert Recorde; of Dee's pupil, Thomas Digges; and of Giordano Bruno, between the 1550s and 80s, all contributed to an incorporation of copernicanism into the discourse of English science.[8] Yet Marlowe continues to write in terms of the old cosmology. The space voyage takes place in a ptolemaic universe. And the disputation between Faustus and Mephostophilis about astronomy in Act II, Scene 2 — 'divine astrology', as Marlowe gets Faustus to call it (line 34) — is made up entirely of precopernican notions. The possibility of heliocentrism, of the daily rotation of the earth, or Bruno's startling concept of an infinite universe with a multiplicity of solar systems are all silently suppressed (lines 33-67).

Instead, Marlowe links the desire for natural knowledge with a desire for power: power of all kinds, and power without limit. In a characteristic move, the space voyage is given a practical purpose. Faustus rests a while. And then, 'mounted . . . upon a dragon's back', 'he now is gone to prove cosmography, / That measures coasts and kingdoms of the earth' (Chorus I, lines 18, 20-1). But, as early as his first speech, Marlowe gives him a remarkable assertion of human ambition. Having rejected established studies — logic, medicine, law, divinity (I. 1. 1-46) — he turns to science. 'These metaphysics of magicians', he declares, '/ And necromantic books are heavenly' (I. 1. 47-8). It could easily be Copernicus that he leafs through: 'Lines, circles, signs, letters and characters: / Ay, these are those that Faustus most desires' (I. 1. 49-50). Then the ambition:

> O what a world of profit and delight,
> Of power, of honour, of omnipotence,
> Is promis'd to the studious artisan!
> All things that move between the quiet poles
> Shall be at my command. Emperors and kings
> Are but obey'd in their several provinces.
> Nor can they raise the wind or rend the clouds.
> But his dominion that exceeds in this
> Stretcheth as far as doth the mind of man:
> A sound magician is a demi-god.
> Here, tire my brains to get a deity.
> (I. 1. 51-61)

In this, Marlowe is representative. For, from early on, the rise
of science was connected with a search for power. From the
humanist abbot, Trithemius, who claimed that 'study generates
knowledge; knowledge bears love; love, likeness; likeness,
communion; communion, virtue; virtue, dignity; dignity, power;
and power performs the miracle'.[9] To the theorist of empirical
method itself, Francis Bacon, the purpose of whose proposed
scientific academy was 'the knowledge of causes, and secret
motions of things; and the enlarging of the bounds of human
empire, to the effecting of all things possible'.[10] The play is
discursively continuous with this tradition. Yet, crucially, it is also
discontinuous; and different, not only from the utopianism of
Bacon, but also from the idealism of Trithemius.

According to the dominant discourse, knowledge of nature was the
knowledge sought by Adam and Eve. It was a sign of pride.
'Knowledge puffeth up', said St Paul in the first letter to the
Corinthians (VIII. 1). The proper study of mankind was the
'mystery of God . . . and of Christ: in whom are hid all the
treasures of wisdom and knowledge' (Letter to the Colossians II. 2-
3). To search out the secrets of nature was to seek the devil.
Literally, since nature was where the devil lived. After their fall, as
Hooker put it, writing about the same time as the play, the devils
were 'dispersed some in the air, some on the earth, some in the
water, some amongst the minerals, dens, and caves, that are under
the earth'.[11]

From this side of the scientific revolution, it is an
extraordinary view to hold. But it was both learned and popular:
present not only in Hooker, but also in the *History* of Faustus,
where it had the status of fact.[12] And it is present in Marlowe.
Almost immediately after his speech on omnipotence, the good
angel exhorts Faustus to put down his 'damned' book, which is
'blasphemy', and read scripture; while the bad angel encourages
him to proceed in 'that famous art', in which 'all nature's treasury' is

to be found. 'Be thou on earth', he says to him, 'as Jove is in the
sky, / Lord and commander of these elements' (I. 1. 68-75);
echoing Satan's words to Eve: 'When ye shall eat thereof, your
eyes shall be opened, and ye shall be as gods' (Genesis III. 5).
Natural knowledge is presented by the text as a temptation to be
resisted. And left to himself, Faustus is represented as luxuriating
in a sense of coming power. It is a representation of a self-
indulgence that is at once reckless and absurd, despite the powerful
empathy of the writing:

> How am I glutted with conceit of this!
> Shall I make spirits fetch me what I please,
> Resolve me of all ambiguities,
> Perform what desperate enterprise I will?
> I'll have them fly to India for gold,
> Ransack the ocean for orient pearl,
> And search all corners of the new-found world
> For pleasant fruits and princely delicates;
> I'll have them read me strange philosophy,
> And tell the secrets of all foreign kings;
> I'll have them wall all Germany with brass,
> And make swift Rhine circle fair Wittenberg;
> I'll have them fill the public schools with silk,
> Wherewith the students shall be bravely clad;
> I'll levy soldiers with the coin they bring,
> And chase the Prince of Parma from our land,
> And reign sole king of all the provinces.
> Yea, stranger engines for the brunt of war
> Than was the fiery keel at Antwerp's bridge
> I'll make my servile spirits to invent.
>   (I. 1. 76-95)

Marlowe, moreover, carefully frames the drama with the
chorus. In the historical prologue, there is no criticism of Faustus's
social rising — the typical experience of Marlowe and his audience:

> Now is he born, of parents base of stock,
> In Germany, within a town called Rhode.
> At riper years to Wittenberg he went,
> Whereas his kinsmen chiefly brought him up.
> So much he profits in divinity,
> The fruitful plot of scholarism grac'd,
> That shortly he was grac'd with doctor's name,
> Excelling all whose sweet delight disputes
> In heavenly matters of theology.
>
> (Chorus, lines 11-19)

But the challenge to ultimate authority entailed in the search for natural knowledge is treated differently. 'Till', the chorus proceeds:

> swol'n with cunning, of a self-conceit,
> His waxen wings did mount above his reach,
> And melting, heavens conspir'd his overthrow.
>
> (Chorus, lines 20-2)

It is denied; and denied in terms of the dominant discourse:

> For falling to a devilish exercise,
> And glutted now with learning's golden gifts,
> He surfeits upon cursed necromancy;
> Nothing so sweet as magic is to him,
> Which he prefers before his chiefest bliss.
>
> (Chorus, lines 23-7)

In the epilogue, the play's action is moralised:

> Faustus is gone: regard his hellish fall,
> Whose fiendful fortune may exhort the wise
> Only to wonder at unlawful things,
> Whose deepness doth entice such forward wits,

To practise more than heavenly power permits.
                                        (Chorus, lines 4 to the end)

Diegesis is homologous with narrative.[13]

There is, nevertheless, a more fundamental derivation from history
than this. Marlowe is very careful to present Faustus with
opportunities for amendment. Effectively, they are the moments
that structure the narrative. And they begin even before Faustus
succumbs to the temptation of natural knowledge in the conjuring
of Mephostophilis in Act I, Scene 3. There is the intervention of
the good and bad angels near the beginning of the play, when
Faustus is warned by the good angel not to read the book of magic,
'lest it tempt thy soul, / And heap God's heavy wrath upon thy head'
(I. 1. 69-70). There is the moment, not long after the conjuring,
when the angels reappear (II. 1. 1-21). There are the two occasions
at the writing of the deed of gift, when Faustus's blood congeals —
an invention of Marlowe's — and when he sees '*Homo fuge!*'
inscribed on his arm (II. 1. 61-9, 76-81). And, in the next scene,
there are the two entrances of the angels, while Faustus and
Mephostophilis are quarrelling (II. 2. 1-17, 67-82).

    Then, towards the end of the drama, near the conclusion of the
middle scenes of travel and adventure, comes a sudden moment of
desperation on Faustus's part (IV. 4. 18-23). It too is an invention of
Marlowe's. And it comes halfway through the trick played on the
horse-courser: one of Faustus's 'merry jests' as the *History* calls them
(Chapter 44) in which, among other things, Faustus and
Mephostophilis are temporarily transformed into protestant heroes
(III. 1-2). It is a moment intensified by the abrupt contrast with the
surrounding comic action, and by an unexpected shift from prose to
verse.[14] This is followed three scenes later, at the beginning of the
climactic Act V, by the appearance of the old man who, as one of his
functions, takes on the role of the good angel (V. 1. 36-67). This is
succeeded, in turn, by the solicitude of the three scholars (V. 2. 24-

79); and, finally, by Faustus's great concluding speech, as the clock
strikes first eleven, then the half-hour, then twelve, and Faustus is
damned: dragged off to hell by the devils (V. 2. 126 to the end).

Structurally, the drama is intertextual with the feudal morality
plays: with their alternation of serious and comic scenes, their
suppression of characters, and their psychomachy.[15] And, like them,
Marlowe emphasises the constant possibility of salvation. 'Yet
Faustus', affirms the second scholar on the brink of Faustus's
damnation, 'look up to heaven, and remember God's mercy is
infinite' (V. 2. 37-8). The morality plays, in fact, go to considerable
lengths to ensure the salvation of their protagonist. In the *Castle of
Perseverance*, right at the beginning of the tradition, Mankind dies
unsaved. But, in a remarkable moment, his soul emerges from under
his deathbed to continue the struggle.[16] Grace is not a key word in
Marlowe's text. But it is a key concept. And the implication is that,
at each of these junctures — even at the congealing of Faustus's
blood — God's grace is being made available for amendment. The
old man is quite explicit about this. And, as another of his functions,
he is a representation of christian steadfastness, and of the
inviolability of faith. 'O stay, good Faustus', he exclaims, as Faustus
goes to kill himself with the dagger, 'stay thy desperate steps!':

> I see an angel hovers o'er thy head,
> And with a vial full of precious grace,
> Offers to pour the same into thy soul.
>   (V. 1. 58-61)[17]

On each occasion, however, Faustus is represented as
rejecting the grace that is offered. He 'excludes' it from his soul, as
the text makes the old man express it later (V. 1. 118). Indeed, after
the initial temptation by the bad angel (I. 1. 72-5) and after the
conjuring two scenes later, the sense of the drama is that Faustus is
unable to accept the grace that is offered. There is even a sense
that, before the temptation, Faustus's free will is compromised.
Near the end of the play, following the intervention by the scholars,

the text has Mephostophilis assert that, when Faustus was 'i'the way to heaven' — about to accept grace — he 'damm'd up' his passage; but also that, when Faustus took up the bible and dismissed divinity (I. 1. 37-46), it was actually Mephostophilis who 'turn'd the leaves' and 'led' his eye (V. 2. 86-9).

Nevertheless, the old man perseveres. 'Then', he exhorts Faustus with the dagger in his hand, 'call for mercy and avoid despair' (V. 1. 62). And Faustus's words a short while after express the psychological contradiction, and the distress, of somebody who desperately wants to alter their condition, but is unable to do so. 'Accursed Faustus', he cries to himself, 'where is mercy now?':

> I do repent, and yet I do despair.
> Hell strives with grace for conquest in my breast.

And the hopelessness of his situation is registered in a question that the text has no answer to. 'What', he asks:

> shall I do to shun the snares of death?
> (V. 1. 68-71)

This sense that choices are not straightforwardly free, and that, once made, they cannot be redeemed, runs strongly counter to the ideology inherited by the sixteenth century. In the *Castle of Perseverance*, Mankind is finally saved by uttering one sentence: 'I put me in God's mercy' (line 3031). And a century later, Everyman is effectively saved by his own efforts. When he dies, his good deeds 'make all sure' (*Everyman*, line 889).[18] It is a sense that is amplified and intensified in Faustus's last speech (V. 2. 126 to the end). In the self-negating energies of line 138, with 'O I'll leap up to my God!' denied by another unanswered question, 'Who pulls me down?'. In the determinism foregrounded in terms of contemporary science in lines 151-2: the apostrophe to the 'stars that reign'd at my nativity, / Whose influence hath allotted death and hell'. In the notion of God as separate from the human sympathies of Christ: as a remote, unforgiving father (lines 139-42, 144-8, 159-64, 181). And in the representation of stifled panic near the conclusion of the speech: 'My God, my God!' — momentarily engendering pity — 'Look not so fierce on me. / Adders and serpents, let me breathe awhile' (lines 181-2).[19]

But the final sense of the speech is that, for his error, Faustus deserves his fate. There is no discursive difference here between the *History* and the play. The time, moreover, for Faustus's amendment is past. 'Ugly hell', he exclaims, 'gape not! Come not, Lucifer! / I'll burn my books'. And the speech concludes with a horrified recognition that what Mephostophilis really is is a tormentor. 'Ah, Mephostophilis!', he cries out, as he steps forward from among the devils to carry him offstage to hell (lines 183 to the end).

The play is situated, not within the ideological formation of feudal christianity, as inflected in the voluntarism of the morality tradition, but within that of sixteenth-century protestantism; specifically, within its later and most radical inflection of calvinism. The form of the drama is consequently transmuted from one that is essentially optimistic — determinedly so — to one that is tragic. The protagonist is not saved, but irredeemably lost. Calvin was quite unequivocal about his position. 'God', he wrote:

> once established by his eternal and unchangeable plan those whom he long before determined once for all to receive into salvation, and those whom, on the other hand, he would devote to destruction . . . with respect to the elect, this plan was founded upon his freely given mercy, without regard to human worth; but by his just and irreprehensible but incomprehensible judgment he has barred the door of life to those whom he has given over to damnation.
>
> (*Institutes of the Christian Religion*, III. 21. 7)[20]

It is a position that openly embraces contradiction. On the one hand, people are responsible for their actions. But on the other, the outcome of their actions is determined by factors beyond their will. And although, in its acceptance of the absolute will of the sovereign father, the position is compatible with contemporary structures of monarchy and hierarchy, it is really an ideology of radical individualism, deriving from the historical experience of the bourgeoisie. In the last analysis, the subject is answerable only to themself; though the characteristic emphasis is upon external constraint. As Engels put it, with a nicely deconstructive irony, 'Predestination . . . was the religious expression of the fact that in the commercial world of competition success or failure does not depend upon a man's activity or cleverness, but upon circumstances uncontrollable by him. It is not of him that willeth or of him that runneth, but of the mercy of unknown superior economic powers'.[21]

Half a dozen years earlier, the first part of *Tamburlaine* had registered the sense of liberation, exhilaration even, engendered by the new economy, with its conviction that Tamburlaine was one of God's chosen: his scourge. *Doctor Faustus*, by contrast, registers the sense of inexorable constriction also engendered by it.[22]

Chapter Six

Hero and Leander: Love and Fate

Hero and Leander is different from the other works Marlowe wrote after he moved to London. Probably written in 1593, it is not a drama meant for the capital's bourgeois audience, but a narrative poem most likely intended, like Shakespeare's *Venus and Adonis*, for presentation to a patron and for publication. It is intended for private reading, not public performance. And it has a strong authorial presence.[1]

The poem is different, too, in its textuality. It is intertextual not with history, but with another humanist resource: classical myth. And the story of Hero and Leander would have been well known to its privileged, educated readership: not only from Ovid's dramatisation of it in the *Heroides* (XVIII and XIX), but also from Musaeus's version of it in *Hero and Leander*, both of which were widely read in the renaissance.[2]

Marlowe constructs a discourse out of Musaeus that is at once comic and tragic. In the Greek writer, Hero is 'unschooled in love's ways' (line 31). And Marlowe develops this into a major theme of his narrative. Hero is 'with love unacquainted' (II. 1). Leander is 'a novice' in love's ways (II. 13). He is 'rude in love, and raw' (II. 61), and has yet to learn 'all that elder lovers know' (II. 69). And it is the disparity between young love and an adult perspective, between remembered innocence and present experience, that leads to the characteristic ironies of the text.[3]

The resultant complexities are at their most evident in the description of Hero and Leander's lovemaking in Sestiad II. It is a description that constitutes the culmination and conclusion of Marlowe's poem. And it corresponds to the drowning of Leander and the suicide of Hero in Musaeus (lines 293 to the end).[4] Leander knocks and calls out at Hero's tower, having just swum the Hellespont (lines 227-31). Hero is more pleased than 'nymphs and shepherds when the timbrel rings', or 'crooked dolphin' when Arion sang at sea (lines 231-4). Marlowe is charmingly pastoral at this point. And Hero 'stayed not for her robes, but straight arose, / And drunk with gladness to the door she goes' (lines 235-6). 'Where', Marlowe continues:

> seeing a naked man, she screeched for fear;
> Such sights as this to tender maids are rare;
> And ran into the dark herself to hide.
> (II. 237-9)

The comic reversal in line 237 stems from the contradictoriness perceived in the inexperienced Hero's emotions. At one moment, she is seen as ecstatically happy: 'drunk with gladness' (line 236); the next, terrified: screeching with 'fear' (line 237). In both instances, she is presented with typically Marlovian exaggeration: 'drunk', 'screeched'. And she is viewed, in a direct authorial intervention characteristic of the poem, with a witty worldliness available only to an elder lover; a worldliness Marlowe found in Ovid. 'Such sights as this', he comments knowingly, 'to tender maids are rare' (line 238).[5]

The wit is saved from cynicism, however, by the pity generated in the text for Hero's predicament. The relationship between her and Leander is seen in traditionally hierarchical terms. He is dominant. She is submissive. And Marlowe never questions this. But Leander is also perceived as predatory, and Hero as a victim. There is a

decisive change of tone in the description at line 259: 'His hands he
cast upon her like a snare'. Hero's reaction combines absurdity,
partly felt in the comic rhyme of lines 261-2 and the parody of
Spenserian language in line 266, with a delicate pathos:

> She, overcome with shame and sallow fear,
> Like chaste Diana when Actaeon spied her,
> Being suddenly betrayed, dived down to hide her.
> And as her silver body downward went,
> With both her hands she made the bed a tent,
> And in her own mind thought herself secure,
> O'ercast with dim and darksome coverture.
>   (II. 260-6)

And the text moves towards the central moment of the
description, which is also a key moment in the work as a whole
(lines 283-96). Leander continues with his advances. And Hero —
also, to an extent, Leander — begins to gain sexual knowledge. 'And
every kiss to her', writes Marlowe, 'was as a charm, / And to Leander
as a fresh alarm' (lines 283-4). And the knowledge gained is
revealed to the reader as essentially tragic. The truce between the
two lovers of line 278 is broken. And Hero 'alas', says Marlowe, '/
(Poor silly maiden)' — pitiful, naive girl — 'at his mercy was' (lines
285-6). Then there is an open authorial interpretation. 'Love',
Marlowe notes:

> is not full of pity (as men say)
> But deaf and cruel where he means to prey.
>   (II. 287-8)

Sexuality is seen to be inexorable. In particular, lovemaking itself
is presented as a violent predation of one partner by another. In
fact, it is virtually equated with killing, in the powerful image of
wringing a bird's neck in lines 289-91. 'Even as a bird', Marlowe
declares:

> which in our hands we wring,
> Forth plungeth, and oft flutters with her wing,
> She trembling strove.
>
> (II. 289-91)

But, in a further perception of contradiction, 'this strife' of Hero's, Marlowe goes on, '(like that / Which made the world) another world begat / Of unknown joy' (lines 291-3). Her awakening sexual experience is viewed in terms of the Greek philosopher Empedocles' idea that all natural change is the result of two opposing forces, strife and love. And Marlowe's implied acceptance of this as an explanation of the origin of the universe, although delivered in an aside, is nevertheless profoundly subversive of the established account of creation in the first two chapters of Genesis.

Marlowe then returns to his Ovidian mode, again focusing on contradiction: on the hypocrisy represented as distinctive of women in matters of sexuality, but also felt implicitly as emanating from their subordinate position. 'Treason was in her thought', he states:

> And cunningly to yield herself she sought.
> Seeming not won, yet won she was at length,
> In such wars women use but half their strength.
>
> (II. 293-6)

The act of sex takes place in lines 297-300. And the narration becomes very remote from the experience being talked about, which is seen to be fundamentally a moment of male activity:

> Leander now, like Theban Hercules,
> Entered the orchard of th'Hesperides,
> Whose fruit none rightly can describe but he
> That pulls or shakes it from the golden tree.
>
> (II. 297-300)

Hero gains greater sexual awareness. There is more contradiction. 'And now', says Marlowe, 'she wished this night were never done' (line 301). And sexual love, though judged to be basically tragic, is also conceived, as in Musaeus, to be life-giving. In Musaeus, love is even able to transcend death (lines 342 to the end). In this poem, Hero 'sighed to think upon th'approaching sun' (line 302). For:

> much it grieved her that the bright daylight
> Should know the pleasure of this blessed night.
> (II. 303-4)

And the description concludes with an affirmation of sexuality through moments of great physical loveliness in the text. There is the image of the two lovers as 'like Mars and Erycine displayed, / Both in each other's arms chained as they laid' (lines 305-6), despite the tragic implications of 'chained'. And there is the poem's final view of Hero (lines 317-26). It is presented as Leander's view, which Marlowe invites the — presumably male — reader to share. Her beauty is conveyed in a conceit as more vital than sunlight:

> Thus near the bed she blushing stood upright,
> And from her countenance behold ye might
> A kind of twilight break, which through the hair,
> As from an orient cloud, glims here and there.
> And round about the chamber this false morn
> Brought forth the day before the day was born.
> (II. 317-22)

And her nakedness is endorsed as more valuable than material wealth, which is associated by the text in the reference to Dis, god both of wealth and of the underworld, with an antihuman miserliness. 'So', Marlowe ends the description:

> Hero's ruddy cheek Hero betrayed,
> And her all naked to his sight displayed,

> Whence his admiring eyes more pleasure took
> Than Dis on heaps of gold fixing his look.
>   (II. 323-6)[6]

Although Hero and Leander are depicted as young, adolescent lovers, their love is, all the same, put forward as representative, even archetypal. The effect of the authorial interventions is, quite deliberately, to generalise and universalise the experience being handled. The text aims to disclose the essence of human love. In particular, it embraces not only heterosexual, but also homosexual, male-to-male relationships. And it makes no fundamental distinction between them.

As Leander swims the Hellespont to reach Hero immediately before the description of their lovemaking, he himself is made love to by Neptune (II. 155-226). It is an episode not found in Ovid, where Neptune is definitely heterosexual, or in Musaeus; and is an invention of Marlowe's.[7] It is a tale of unrequited love, in which Leander plays Hero's part; and Neptune, Leander's. When Leander leaps into the water, Neptune imagines it is Ganymede, the beautiful cupbearer of Jupiter, who has left heaven. Leander is so desirable — is the implication. At the end of the sixteenth century, 'Ganymede' was a codeword for a young homosexual.[8] And 'the lusty god embraced him, called him love, / And swore he never should return to Jove' (lines 167-8). Even the waves desire him. In a witty image, they 'mounted up, intending to have kissed him, / And fell in drops like tears because they missed him' (lines 173-4), as Neptune beats them down with his mace.

The pathos and absurdity are here felt in relation to Leander who:

> being up, began to swim,
> And, looking back, saw Neptune follow him;
> Whereat aghast, the poor soul 'gan to cry,
> 'O let me visit Hero ere I die.'
>   (II. 175-8)

And Marlowe resumes the witty imagery in a passage that describes the movement of water round a swimmer's body, just as the previous image had depicted the breaking of the waves, but which is also a frank description of homosexual lovemaking; though, teasingly, he omits the most erotic caresses. Neptune 'clapped' Leander's 'plump cheeks', and:

> with his tresses played,
> And smiling wantonly, his love bewrayed.
> He watched his arms, and as they opened wide
> At every stroke, betwixt them would he slide
> And steal a kiss, and then run out and dance,
> And as he turned, cast many a lustful glance,
> And threw him gaudy toys to please his eye,
> And dive into the water, and there pry
> Upon his breast, his thighs, and every limb,
> And up again, and close beside him swim,
> And talk of love.

> (II. 181-91)

There is the same distance between youthful innocence and adult experience, this time in terms of homosexual passion, and on this occasion presented ironically. To Neptune's words of love 'Leander made reply'. "'You are deceived'", he said, "'I am no woman, I'". 'Thereat smiled Neptune' (lines 191-3).

Marlowe, moreover, gives Neptune a story to recount which, affectively, communicates a deep sense of the poignancy of human desire. The story focuses in particular on homosexual desire. And it constitutes a very Marlovian use of pastoral. Neptune tells:

> How that a shepherd, sitting in a vale,
> Played with a boy so fair and kind,
> As for his love both earth and heaven pined;
> That of the cooling river durst not drink,

Lest water-nymphs should pull him from the brink;
And when he sported in the fragrant lawns,
Goat-footed satyrs and up-staring fauns
Would steal him thence.
                              (II. 194-201)

Leander, however, is indifferent to Neptune's advances.
And Neptune's mood darkens. The text once more reveals the
tragic insistence of sexuality (lines 207-9). There is an
absurdity in Neptune's sudden change of heart as love then
makes him relent (lines 209-10). And the wound inflicted on
his hand conveys the inescapable pain of personal relationships
(lines 211-12). 'Neptune', writes Marlowe, 'was angry' that
Leander:

                              gave no ear,
And in his heart revenging malice bare:
He flung at him his mace, but as it went,
He called it in, for love made him repent.
The mace returning back, his own hand hit,
As meaning to be venged for darting it.
                              (II. 207-12)

The pathos of the narrative now centres on Neptune, who
misreads Leander's ordinary human pity for his wound as love.
And Marlowe intervenes in the story in order to generalise from
this, and so foreground what is presented as the essentially tragic
uncertainty at the heart of sexual experience. 'Love', he
pronounces, 'is too full of faith, too credulous, / With folly and
false hope deluding us' (lines 221-2). And in one of the sudden
modulations of tone characteristic of the whole work, the
pessimism latent in this observation shifts to the near-cynicism
of the Ovidian wit that the episode concludes with. Neptune
rushes off to the ocean floor to find presents that will captivate
Leander's affections. "Tis wisdom to give much', Marlowe notes

finally, 'a gift   prevails / When deep persuading oratory fails'
(lines 225-6).

The text constructs a male homosexual subjectivity; a subjectivity
evidenced earlier in Marlowe. Musaeus gives a description of Hero
near the beginning of his work (lines 55-66). And Marlowe follows
him in this. In fact, he virtually begins the poem with a portrait of
her (I. 5-50). But Marlowe also adds a description of Leander, to
which there is no corresponding passage in Musaeus, or in Ovid.
The portrait of Hero is external. It is largely of her clothes. And
Marlowe presents her as a typical renaissance princess or great lady.[9]
The description of Leander, which comes next in the narrative, is
very different in character (I. 51-90). It is predominantly physical
and highly erotic. 'His body', Marlowe declares:

>   was as straight as Circe's wand;
>   Jove might have sipped out nectar from his hand.
>   Even as delicious meat is to the taste,
>   So was his neck in touching, and surpassed
>   The white of Pelops' shoulder. I could tell ye
>   How smooth his breast was, and how white his belly,
>   And whose immortal fingers did imprint
>   That heavenly path with many a curious dint
>   That runs along his back.
>   (I. 61-9)

Especially powerful in creating a sense of sexual pleasure is the
synaesthesia of lines 63-4, with their comparison of touching flesh
to tasting food.

Apart, however, from the reference to 'succeeding times' in
line 54, and the implicit likening of him in lines 59-60 to
Endymion, who was loved by Cynthia the moon, Leander is seen
exclusively in terms of his attractiveness to men. Jason and the
Argonauts, says Marlowe, with the nice hyperbole that is

characteristic of the description, would have hazarded more for his 'dangling tresses' than they did for the golden fleece (lines 55-8). Jupiter, the chief of the gods, would have drunk from a cup held in his hand: the Ganymede motif once more (line 62). And if 'wild Hippolytus', devoted to chastity and hunting, had seen him, Marlowe claims, 'enamoured of his beauty had he been' (lines 77-8). For Leander's 'presence' affected the least cultivated. It 'made the rudest peasant melt, / That in the vast uplandish country dwelt' (lines 79-80). Even the 'barbarous Thracian soldier', an archetype in classical times of masculine brutality and inhumanity — 'moved with nought', as Marlowe puts it — 'was moved with him, and for his favour sought' (lines 81-2).[10]

The passage is clearly a reworking, in more openly sexual terms, of the celebration of Tamburlaine by Menaphon in *Tamburlaine*, Part I (II. 1. 7-30). And it is manifestly a reworking too, at a more conscious level, of Faustus's eulogy of Helen of Troy near the end of *Doctor Faustus*, where the praise of her beauty slips uncontrolledly into comparisons of her with men (V. 1. 97-116). Instead of being compared to Semele or Arethusa, both of them women, she is likened to their male lovers: to Jupiter and to Apollo, the 'monarch of the sky'. 'Brighter art thou', Marlowe makes Faustus say to her:

> than flaming Jupiter,
> When he appear'd to hapless Semele:
> More lovely than the monarch of the sky,
> In wanton Arethusa's azur'd arms.
>
> (V. 1. 112-15)

As in *Edward II*, there is no criticism of homosexual relationships. The love that Neptune has for Leander may be tragic, on occasion even absurd. But it is not wrong. And as with the earlier play, this is a position that goes right against the morality of the time. Yet the description of Leander ends with a moment that is even more radical than this.

The dominant ideology of the age assumed that sexual relationships were normally between men and women, and that heterosexual love found its natural expression in marriage. Any other kind of sexuality was a perversion: an 'abomination', as Leviticus termed homosexual relations (XX. 13). And this gender-specific sexuality was subsumed under the larger, in fact all-embracing, discourse of hierarchy. As the monarch was superior to his subjects, so the husband was superior to his wife.[11] Unlike Musaeus who, contradictorily, endorses marriage, yet does not criticise Hero and Leander for making love while unmarried, Marlowe effectively ignores marriage. He certainly does not disapprove of either Hero or Leander for wanting or having sex outside it. Nevertheless, to an extent, the dominant ideology prevails in the poem. Although the relationship between Leander and Hero, like that between Neptune and Leander, is seen as typically predacious, it is also perceived as essentially hierarchical. The male Leander is represented as superior to, more active than, the passive, female Hero; just as the older Neptune dominates the less experienced Leander. Towards the conclusion of the description of Leander, however, the text separates sexuality from gender. 'Some swore', Marlowe writes, that Leander was 'a maid in man's attire', for:

> in his looks were all that men desire,
> A pleasant smiling cheek, a speaking eye,
> A brow for love to banquet royally.
>
> (I. 83-6)

The sentiment here is male-directed. It is a matter of what 'men' desire (line 84); not of what women, or men and women, desire. But in place of the gender-specific sexuality of the dominant discourse, the lines affirm a sexuality that is free to find satisfaction in either gender. It makes no difference whether Leander is male or female. In his beauty men are able to find everything they are looking for.

And the description closes with an endorsement of sexual love: 'love's holy fire' as Marlowe expresses it later (I. 193), or 'the rites of most wise Cythereia' as, with basically the same affirmation, Musaeus called the lovemaking of Hero and Leander in his poem (line 273). Those who knew that Leander was a man, says Marlowe — homosexual orientation again — would urge him to make love. '"Leander"', they would declare, '"thou art made for amorous play: / Why art thou not in love?"' (lines 88-9). Then Marlowe adds: '"and loved of all?"' (line 89). Not 'why are you not married?'. But 'why are you not available to everyone, regardless of gender?'.

And Marlowe finishes with an exhortation, which is both reported within the narrative as being spoken to Leander and addressed directly to the reader, who is assumed to be male. '"Though thou be fair"', Marlowe writes, '"yet be not thine own thrall"' (line 90). Do not be like Narcissus, the beautiful young man of mythology who figures a little earlier in the description (lines 73-6), who 'leapt into the water for a kiss / Of his own shadow' (lines 74-5), and drowned; and who became a powerful symbol of self-love and autoeroticism. Here he is also used to signify a human waste. 'Despising many', Marlowe asserts, he 'died ere he could enjoy the love of any' (lines 75-6). Sexuality is to be shared, is the implication of the text. 'For', as Marlowe maintains later in the poem, 'from the earth to heaven is Cupid raised, / Where fancy is in equal balance peised' (II. 31-2). It is to be shared without reference to the form a relationship takes: whether married or unmarried. And it is to be shared irrespective of gender. Taken together, lines 83-90 of the description constitute a moment that is deeply disintegrative of the morality of the time.

More is involved, however, in Marlowe's sense of the fundamentally tragic nature of human love in the poem than the relentlessness of sexual desire, or the uncertainty felt to exist deep in personal relationships. Musaeus emphasised the irresistibility of love.   When Leander first meets Hero, Musaeus addresses him directly.[12]   'But you, dread-suffering Leander', he says, 'when you saw the glorious girl, / You had no will to consume your heart with secret goadings, / But':

> vanquished, all unlooked-for, by the fire-smitten
> arrows
> You had no will to live in loss of lovely Hero.
> (Lines 86-9)

'Out of the eye's glances', he turns to say to the reader, '/ Beauty glides, and journeys into the hearts of men' (lines 94-5).   And early in the first sestiad of *Hero and Leander*, Marlowe theorises quite explicitly about the coerciveness of love (lines 167-76).   'It lies not in our power', he pronounces:

> to love or hate,
> For will in us is overruled by fate.
> (I. 167-8)

And he continues with an image of two runners stripped to the waist — a hint of homoeroticism — and about to race against each other:

> When two are stripped, long ere the course begin
> We wish that one should lose, the other win.
> (I. 169-70)

Then an image of two indistinguishable gold bars:

> And one especially do we affect
> Of two gold ingots like in each respect.
> The reason no man knows.
> (I. 171-3)

Love is not only coercive. It is also irrational. There is no explanation for one preference rather than another. And Marlowe rests on the proverbial notion, going back to Plato and shared by Musaeus, that love enters through the eyes, not through the mind. In a way that is representative of the poem, he epigrammatises, and so intensifies, the idea (line 176). 'Let it suffice', he concludes:

> What we behold is censured by our eyes.
> Where both deliberate, the love is slight;
> Who ever loved, that loved not at first sight?
>   (I. 173-6)[13]

There is, furthermore, a feeling in the poem that love is doomed to failure, whether consummated, as in the case of Hero and Leander, or unreciprocated, as with Leander and Neptune. Like Ovid and Musaeus before him, Marlowe assumes that the tragic outcome of the story is known by the reader. And he refers to it at the outset, in the poem's very first line. The Hellespont is said to be 'guilty of true love's blood' (I. 1): guilty of the deaths of Hero and Leander. And although the narrative breaks off before the outcome is reached, the poem nevertheless finishes with a moment that is heavy with tragic foreboding, and which, in effect, concludes the story (II. 327 to the end). It is a foreboding that is strongly present in Ovid. And it comes, strikingly, after the affirmation of human love through Hero's nakedness (II. 323-6), in one of the radical shifts of mood that are typical of the text. Dawn breaks. And the planet Venus 'mocks' the night, which only recently had been 'blessed' (II. 304), life-enhancing; but which now is abruptly represented as an 'ugly' woman. In a male-centred way, the planet is conceived as a young man, Hesperus, 'with his flaring beams'. And Night, declares Marlowe, bringing the poem to a close:

> o'ercome with anguish, shame and rage,
> Danged down to hell her loathsome carriage.
>   (II. 332 to the end)

The transcendence of love in Musaeus, with its final triumph over death, finds no echo in Marlowe.

Part, too, of the meaning of the Mercury episode at the conclusion of Sestiad I (lines 386 to the end), which is not in Musaeus and which was invented by Marlowe, is that circumstances are adverse to the happy success of love; just as they are to the recognition and reward of individual talent. The Destinies, 'on whom heaven, earth, and hell relies' (line 443), have only hatred for Love, and refuse even to answer his request that Hero and Leander 'might enjoy each other, and be blest' (I. 380); in the same way that 'to this day' — to 1593 — 'is every scholar poor', and 'few great lords in virtuous deeds' do 'joy' (lines 471, 479). The complaint about the inadequacies of contemporary patronage, with which the episode practically ends (lines 463-82), is highly characteristic of the 1590s; and forms a moment of considerable power in the text.[14] As in *Doctor Faustus*, the writing evinces a personal pessimism that is inseparable from a wider, social despondency, though here there is a double displacement: from the experience of the new economy to that of patronage as well as of intimate relationships.

Marlowe is representative of that fraction of the Elizabethan middle class which felt its interest to be identical with that of the monarchy. That fraction was the dominant one in the half-dozen years around 1590 when Marlowe was writing. And it is from this contradictory class position — bourgeois, yet committed to the monarchical advantage — that the characteristic tensions and contradictions of Marlowe's work stem. The radical individualism of *Tamburlaine*, Part I, becomes tempered in Part II by a notion of limit, inherent in the traditional ideology espoused by the monarchy, into a naturalistic stoicism. In the *Jew of Malta*, the economic individualism that was at the heart of the sixteenth-century bourgeoisie is rejected, ridiculed even, in favour of the current social order represented in Ferneze. In *Edward II*, political individualism as well as feudal particularism is curbed and denied, to the benefit of the crown, in the struggle between Mortimer and the two Edwards. And in *Doctor Faustus*, the spirit of individual inquiry, once championed with such bravura in the first part of *Tamburlaine*, is crushed in the damnation of Faustus, on behalf of the ideological conservatism embraced by Elizabeth. Only the sexual radicalism of *Hero and Leander*, developed from the acceptance of homosexuality in *Edward II*, and envisaging personal relationships without restriction, remained at Marlowe's death out of the original individualism, which saw no boundary of any kind to human aspiration.[15]

Notes

Preface

1   On the variety of critical positions now available see Terry Eagleton, *Marxism and Literary Criticism* (London, 1976) and *Literary Theory* (Oxford, 1983); and Roger Webster, *Studying Literary Theory* (London, 1990).

Chapter 1: Life and Context

1   *The Tragicall History of Christopher Marlowe*, 2 vols (1942; reprinted Hamden, Connecticut, 1964), I, 92.

2   Quoted from Bakeless, *Tragicall History*, I, 77.

3   See S. Schoenbaum, *William Shakespeare: A Compact Documentary Life*, revised edition (Oxford, 1987), and R.C. Bald, *John Donne: A Life* (Oxford, 1970).

4   Biographical details are taken mostly from Bakeless. But see also Frederick S. Boas, *Christopher Marlowe*, revised edition (Oxford, 1953); R.B. Wernham, 'Christopher Marlowe at Flushing in 1592', *English Historical Review*, 91 (1976), 344-5; Constance Brown Kuriyama, *Hammer or Anvil* (New Brunswick, 1980), pp. 213-32, 'Marlowe, Shakespeare, and the Nature of Biographical Evidence', *University of Hartford Studies in Literature*, 20 (1988), 1-12,

and 'Marlowe's Nemesis: The Identity of Richard Baines', in *'A Poet and a filthy Play-maker'*, edited by Kenneth Friedenreich et al. (New York, 1988), pp. 343-60; A.L. Rowse, *Christopher Marlowe*, revised edition (London, 1981); and William Urry, *Christopher Marlowe and Canterbury* (London, 1988).

5   See Maurice Dobb, *Studies in the Development of Capitalism*, revised edition (London, 1963); Peter Kriedte, *Peasants, Landlords and Merchant Capitalists* (Leamington Spa, 1983); Colin Mooers, *The Making of Bourgeois Europe* (London, 1991); H.G. Koenigsberger, George L. Mosse, and G.Q. Bowler, *Europe in the Sixteenth Century*, second edition (London, 1989); Christopher Hill, *Reformation to Industrial Revolution*, revised edition (Harmondsworth, 1969); and G.R. Elton, *England Under the Tudors*, third edition (London, 1991). For a theoretical discussion of the historiography of the period see the introduction to *Uses of History: Marxism, Postmodernism and the Renaissance*, edited by Francis Barker, Peter Hulme, and Margaret Iversen (Manchester, 1991), pp. 1-23.

6   Editions of the *Homilies* can be found in *The Two Books of Homilies* (Oxford, 1859) and *Certain Sermons or Homilies (1547) and A Homily against Disobedience and Wilful Rebellion (1570)*, edited by Ronald B. Bond (Toronto, 1987). For the prayer book see F.E. Brightman, *The English Rite*, second edition, 2 vols (1921; reprinted Farnborough, 1970) and *The Book of Common Prayer 1559*, edited by John E. Booty (Charlottesville, 1976). The cultural dislocation of the time is discussed by Hiram Haydn, *The Counter-Renaissance* (New York, 1950); Alan Sinfield, *Literature in Protestant England 1560-1660* (London, 1983); and Jonathan Dollimore, *Radical Tragedy*, second edition (London, 1989).

Chapter 2: *Tamburlaine*

1   On the Elizabethan association of Turkey with Spain see
     Simon Shepherd, *Marlowe and the Politics of Elizabethan
     Theatre* (Brighton, 1986), pp. 142-5. The effects of the
     armada on the plays of the time are discussed by David
     Bevington, *Tudor Drama and Politics* (Cambridge,
     Massachusetts, 1968), pp. 187-95, 209-11. Margot
     Heinemann traces the developing context between 1580 and
     the seventeenth-century revolution in 'Political Drama', in *The
     Cambridge Companion to English Renaissance Drama*, edited
     by A.R. Braunmuller and Michael Hattaway (Cambridge,
     1990), pp. 161-205.

2   For the importance of history within humanism see J.B. Trapp,
     'Education in the Renaissance', in *Background to the English
     Renaissance*, edited by J.B. Trapp (London, 1974), pp. 67-89,
     and Donald R. Kelley, 'The Theory of History', in *The Cambridge
     History of Renaissance Philosophy*, edited by Charles B. Schmitt
     et al. (Cambridge, 1988), pp. 746-61. Extracts from Perondini
     and Whetstone can be found in Cunningham, *Tamburlaine*, pp.
     318-29. Quotation is from this edition.

3   Compare Stephen Greenblatt, *Renaissance Self-Fashioning*
     (Chicago, 1980), pp. 193-4, 223-4, and Catherine Belsey, 'The
     Illusion of Empire: Elizabethan Expansionism and
     Shakespeare's Second Tetralogy', *Literature and History*,
     Second Series, 1, No. 2 (Autumn 1990), 13-21.

4   See J.B. Steane, *Marlowe*, revised edition (Cambridge, 1970),
     pp. 62-116, and L.C. Knights, 'The Strange Case of
     Christopher Marlowe', in *Further Explorations* (London,
     1965), pp. 75-98. The play continued to be acted until the
     middle of the seventeenth century.

5   With the homoeroticism of this moment compare Shepherd,
     Marlowe and the Politics of Elizabethan Theatre, pp. 197-207.
     Marlowe was almost certainly homosexual. See Kuriyama,
     Hammer or Anvil, passim.

6   On feudal discourse see Geoffrey Hughes, *Words in Time* (Oxford, 1988), pp. 32-66.

7   On self-projection in Marlowe see Kuriyama, *Hammer or Anvil*, passim. The Elizabethan audience consisted of all social classes, men and women, but was mainly middle class. See Andrew Gurr, *The Shakespearean Stage 1574-1642*, second edition (Cambridge, 1980), pp. 195-215, and *Playgoing in Shakespeare's London* (Cambridge, 1987), pp. 49-79; and Walter Cohen, *Drama of a Nation* (Ithaca, New York, 1985), pp. 166-70. The play's reception is discussed by Richard Levin, 'The Contemporary Perception of Marlowe's Tamburlaine', in *Medieval and Renaissance Drama in England*, Volume 1, edited by J. Leeds Barroll (New York, 1984), pp. 51-70.

8   The moment is sometimes seen as ironical, the violent spectacle undermining the language: by, for instance, Shepherd, *Marlowe and the Politics of Elizabethan Theatre*, pp. 23-4, 37-8. The position implicit in the argument here is that, on the contrary, the rhetoric *legitimates* the violence. On the connection between Zenocrate, who was an invention of Marlowe's, and Elizabeth in their chastity see Shepherd, pp. 187-8.

9   Donne does something similar at the beginning of James I's reign in the 'Sun Rising'. See my discussion in 'The Poetry of John Donne: Literature, History and Ideology', in *Jacobean Poetry and Prose*, edited by Clive Bloom (London, 1988), pp. 78-95. On the refusal of limit in the sixteenth century see Haydn, *Counter-Renaissance*, pp. 325-460. Recent histories of the rise of individualism are discussed by David Aers, 'Reflections on Current Histories of the Subject', *Literature and History*, Second Series, 2, No. 2 (Autumn, 1991), 20-34. The speech has also been viewed ironically. See, for example, Catherine Belsey, *Critical Practice* (London, 1980), pp. 94-5.

10   The whole question of ideology and discourse is discussed by Terry Eagleton, *Ideology* (London, 1991).

11   On the Elizabethan theatre as an early capitalist formation —
     artisanal base, feudal superstructure — see Cohen, *Drama of a
     Nation*, pp. 136-85.

12   The episode derives from the battle of Varna, fought in 1444
     between Vladislav III and Murad II, in which the papal legate
     absolved Vladislav from his truce with Murad. Vladislav was
     subsequently defeated and killed. Within protestant mythology
     the battle was an archetypal instance of catholic duplicity, and
     would have been familiar to Marlowe's audience. See Roy W.
     Battenhouse, 'Protestant Apologetics and the Subplot of 2
     Tamburlaine', *English Literary Renaissance*, 3 (1973), 30-43.
     In 1587, moreover, 'Sigismund', which is Marlowe's invention,
     is likely to have reminded the audience of Sigismund III, the
     'Polish Philip II' and persecutor of protestants, who became
     king of Poland in August.

13   Accounts of stoicism in the sixteenth century can be found in
     Brian P. Copenhaver and Charles B. Schmitt, *Renaissance
     Philosophy* (Oxford, 1992), pp. 196-284, and Jill Kraye,
     'Moral Philosophy', in *Cambridge History of Renaissance
     Philosophy*, edited by Schmitt et al., pp. 360-74. The revival
     of stoicism in the century dates from the 1580s.

14   The plays have been read in this way: classically, by Roy W.
     Battenhouse, *Marlowe's Tamburlaine*, corrected edition
     (Nashville, 1964).

15   Reference to the bible is to *The Holy Bible . . . the Authorized
     Version* [1611], introduced by Alfred W. Pollard (Oxford,
     1985). Quotation is from *The Geneva Bible* [1560],
     introduced by Lloyd E. Berry (Madison, Milwaukee, 1969).

16   See Johnstone Parr, 'Tamburlaine's Malady' (1944), in
     *Marlowe: Tamburlaine the Great, Edward the Second, and
     The Jew of Malta*, edited by John Russell Brown (London,
     1982), pp. 113-27, and John Henry, 'Doctors and Healers:
     Popular Culture and the Medical Profession', in *Science,
     Culture and Popular Belief in Renaissance Europe*, edited by
     Stephen Pumfrey et al. (Manchester, 1991), pp. 198-9.

17 On the importance of stoicism in the play compare Sinfield, *Literature in Protestant England*, pp. 8l-6.
18 Shepherd makes a similar point, *Marlowe and the Politics of Elizabethan Theatre*, p. 206.

Chapter 3: The *Jew of Malta*

1   These observations derive ultimately from T.S. Eliot's seminal essay, 'Christopher Marlowe' (1919), in *Selected Essays*, third edition (London, 1951), pp. 118-25. The figure of the vice, which dominated English drama in the third quarter of the sixteenth century, is discussed by Peter Happé, '"The Vice" and the Popular Theatre, 1547-80', in *Poetry and Drama 1570-1700*, edited by Antony Coleman and Antony Hammond (London, 1981), pp. 13-31.
2   See Catherine Minshull, 'Marlowe's "Sound Machevill"', in *Renaissance Drama*, New Series, Volume 13, edited by Leonard Barkan (Evanston, 1982), pp. 35-53, and Hughes, *Words in Time*, pp. 186-7.
3   On antisemitic discourse see Wilbur Sanders, *The Dramatist and the Received Idea* (Cambridge, 1968), pp. 339-51, and Hughes, *Words in Time*, pp. 79-80, 244-5.
4   The Geneva bible comments: 'As they wished, so this curse taketh place to this day'.
5   The play's antisemitism is discussed by Jean-Marie Maguin, '*The Jew of Malta*: Marlowe's Ideological Stance and the Play-World's Ethos', *Cahiers Elisabéthains*, 27 (1985), 17-26. It has been denied: especially by Sanders, *Dramatist and the Received Idea*, pp. 38-60, 339-5l.
6   *Machiavelli: The Prince*, edited by Quentin Skinner and Russell Price, corrected edition (Cambridge, 1989), pp. 6l-2. The book was probably written in 1513, and first printed in 1532. Minshull makes the same point, 'Marlowe's "Sound Machevill"', p. 47.

7   For the view, however, that Ferneze's machiavellianism is subversively revealed by Barabas's see Greenblatt, *Renaissance Self-Fashioning*, pp. 203-10.

8   It has been argued, though, that Barabas's enjoyableness as a character induces complicity with him: again by Greenblatt, *Renaissance Self-Fashioning*, pp. 215-16.

9   See lines 1535 to the end in *W. Wager: The Longer Thou Livest and Enough Is as Good as a Feast*, edited by R. Mark Benbow (Lincoln, Nebraska, 1967). The play was written about 1570.

10   On the different possible readings of the play's conclusion see Bob Hodge, 'Marlowe, Marx and Machiavelli: Reading into the Past', in David Aers et al., *Literature, Language and Society in England 1580-1680* (Dublin, 1981), pp. 1-22, and Edward L. Rocklin, 'Marlowe as Experimental Dramatist: The Role of the Audience in *The Jew of Malta*', in '*A Poet and a filthy Play-maker*', edited by Friedenreich et al., pp. 129-42. The play as an imperialist text is discussed by Emily C. Bartels, 'Malta, the Jew, and the Fictions of Difference: Colonialist Discourse in Marlowe's *The Jew of Malta*', *English Literary Renaissance*, 20 (1990), 1-16.

11   No single historical intertext for the play is known. See Bawcutt, *Jew of Malta*, pp. 4-5.

12   See *Thomas More: Utopia* [1516], edited by George M. Logan and Robert M. Adams (Cambridge, 1989), pp. 18-21. The book was probably written in 1515-16.

13   Compare Hodge, 'Marlowe, Marx and Machiavelli', p. 13.

14   On feudal hostility to capitalism see R.H. Tawney, *Religion and the Rise of Capitalism* (1926; reprinted Harmondsworth, 1961); L.C. Knights, *Drama and Society in the Age of Jonson* (1937; reprinted Harmondsworth, 1962); and Don E. Wayne, 'Drama and Society in the Age of Jonson: An Alternative View', in *Renaissance Drama*, edited by Barkan, pp. 103-29.

15   See John Edwards, *The Jews in Christian Europe 1400-1700*, revised edition (London, 1991), and Frances A. Yates,

'Elizabethan England and the Jews', in *The Occult Philosophy in the Elizabethan Age* (London, 1979), pp. 109-14.

16 Quoted by Tawney, *Religion and the Rise of Capitalism*, p. 185.

17 Quotation is from *The Shoemaker's Holiday: Thomas Dekker*, second edition, edited by Anthony Parr (London, 1990). It is likely the play was written in 1599.

18 See John McVeagh, *Tradefull Merchants* (London, 1981).

Chapter 4: *Edward II*

1 For an edition of Holinshed see *Holinshed's Chronicles of England, Scotland, and Ireland*, revised edition, 6 vols (1587; reprinted New York, 1965). All reference is to this text.

2 With the argument being developed here compare James Voss, '*Edward II*: Marlowe's Historical Tragedy', *English Studies*, 63 (1982), 517-30; Cohen, *Drama of a Nation*, pp. 232-9; and Claude J. Summers, 'Sex, Politics, and Self-Realization in *Edward II*', in '*A Poet and a filthy Play-maker*', edited by Friedenreich et al., pp. 221-40.

3 See, for example, I. 1. 100; I. 2. 11, 30; I. 4. 16, 82, 291, 402.

4 On Niobe see *Metamorphoses*, VI. 146-312, in *Ovid in Six Volumes*, Volume 3, edited and translated by Frank Justus Miller, second edition (Cambridge, Massachusetts, 1921).

5 The play shares this structural shift with other plays of the time. See Michael Manheim, 'The Weak King History Play of the Early 1590's', in *Renaissance Drama*, New Series, Volume 2, edited by S. Schoenbaum (Evanston, 1969), pp. 71-80.

6 See Charlton, Waller, and Lees, *Edward II*, pp. 191-2, where the relevant passage is quoted. The episode is not in Holinshed.

7 The stress, all the same, is sometimes seen to be on Edward's common humanity: by, for example, John F. McElroy, 'Repetition, Contrariety, and Individualization in *Edward II*', *Studies in English Literature*, 24 (1984), 205-24. One effect

of the humanisation of monarchy that took place in the 1590s and the first years of the seventeenth century, mostly in Shakespeare, was, paradoxically, its subversion by its desacralisation. See Franco Moretti, 'The Great Eclipse: Tragic Form as the Deconsecration of Sovereignty', in *Signs Taken for Wonders*, revised edition (London, 1988), pp. 42-82.

8   A similar structure can be found in Donne. See my 'Poetry of John Donne', in *Jacobean Poetry and Prose*, edited by Bloom, pp. 78-95. For the view that Edward III's minority questions the stability of the play's ending see Michael Hattaway, *Elizabethan Popular Theatre* (London, 1982), pp. 143-4.

9   See Sharon Tyler, 'Bedfellows Make Strange Politics: Christopher Marlowe's *Edward II*', in *Drama, Sex and Politics* (Cambridge, 1985), pp. 55-68. Kuriyama suggests Edward and his relationships may be modelled on James I and his early affair with Lennox. See *Hammer or Anvil*, pp. 209-10.

10   Quoted from A.L. Rowse, *The Elizabethan Renaissance: The Life of the Society* (1971; reprinted London, 1974), p. 186. On homosexuality in the sixteenth century see Alan Bray, *Homosexuality in Renaissance England* (London, 1982) and 'Homosexuality and the Signs of Male Friendship in Elizabethan England', *History Workshop*, 29 (1990), 1-19; and Bruce R. Smith, *Homosexual Desire in Shakespeare's England* (Chicago, 1991).

11   Compare Summers, 'Sex, Politics, and Self-Realization in *Edward II*', pp. 222-3, and Smith, *Homosexual Desire*, pp. 209-23.

12   On the theory of absolutism, in which James I is an important figure, see John Plamenatz, *Man and Society*, Volume I (London, 1963), pp. 155-208, and *Renaissance Views of Man*, edited by Stevie Davies (Manchester, 1978), pp. 150-78.

Chapter 5: *Doctor Faustus*

1   For an attempt at an ironical reading see Julia Briggs, 'Marlowe's *Massacre at Paris*: A Reconsideration', *Review of English Studies*, New Series, 34 (1983), 257-78.

2   Quoted from a letter of Johannes Trithemius to Johannes Virdung von Hassfurt, dated 20 August 1507, in Philip Mason Palmer and Robert Pattison More, *The Sources of the Faust Tradition* (New York, 1936), pp. 83-6.

3   See Frank Baron, *Doctor Faustus: From History to Legend* (Munich, 1978). Faustus's prediction was apparently accurate. 'I must confess', wrote von Hutten, 'that the philosopher Faust hit the nail on the head, for we struck a very bad year' (letter to Moritz von Hutten, 16 January 1540, quoted in Palmer and More, *Sources*, pp. 95-6).

4   On Copernicus see Angus Armitage, *Copernicus* (New York, 1957), and J.R. Ravetz, 'The Copernican Revolution', in *Companion to the History of Modern Science*, edited by R.C. Olby et al. (London, 1990), pp. 201-16. The *Revolutions* can be found in *Great Books of the Western World*, Volume XVI, edited by Robert Maynard Hutchins (Chicago, 1952). On the rise of science, which was deeply contested, see John A. Schuster, 'The Scientific Revolution', in *Companion to the History of Modern Science*, edited by Olby et al., pp. 217-42, and Roy Porter, Introduction, *Science, Culture and Popular Belief*, edited by Pumfrey et al., pp. 1-15.

5   See Baron, *Doctor Faustus*, in particular pp. 78-9, and 'Georg Lukács on the Origins of the Faust Legend', in *Faust Through Four Centuries*, edited by Peter Boerner and Sidney Johnson (Tübingen, 1989), pp. 13-25; and Keefer, *Doctor Faustus*, pp. xxxvii-xlv.

6   The *Historia von Doctor Johann Fausten* of 1587 has been edited by Stephan Füssel and Hans Joachim Kreutzer (Stuttgart, 1988). The *History*, written by an unknown P.F., can be found in Palmer and More, *Sources*, pp. 134-236. All references are to this edition.

7   On renaissance science see Haydn, *Counter-Renaissance*, pp. 176-292, particularly pp. 186-90; Copenhaver and Schmitt, *Renaissance Philosophy*, pp. 285-328; and R.S. Woolhouse, *The Empiricists* (Oxford, 1988), pp. 9-26. A comparable figure in Elizabethan England, who may have provided a model for Marlowe's character, was John Dee. See Yates, 'Christopher Marlowe on Conjurors, Imperialists and Jews', in *Occult Philosophy*, pp. 115-25, and Peter J. French, *John Dee* (London, 1972).

8   See Armitage, *Copernicus*, pp. 162-204.

9   Quoted from Haydn, *Counter-Renaissance*, pp. 185-6.

10   *New Atlantis* (1627), in *Francis Bacon: The Advancement of Learning and New Atlantis*, edited by Arthur Johnston (Oxford, 1974), p. 239. The work was most likely written in 1603-5.

11   *Richard Hooker: Of the Laws of Ecclesiastical Polity*, edited by Arthur Stephen McGrade (Cambridge, 1989), p. 66 (I. 4. 3). The preface and first four books of the *Laws* were published in 1593.

12   See, in particular, Chapter 18.

13   Alternative readings, however, can be found in Shepherd, *Marlowe and the Politics of Elizabethan Theatre*, pp. 91-109, 134-41, 209, and — most ingeniously — in William Empson, *Faustus and the Censor* (Oxford, 1987).

14   On the connection of these middle scenes with the popular culture of the time see Thomas Pettitt, 'Formulaic Dramaturgy in *Doctor Faustus*', in '*A Poet and a filthy Play-maker*', edited by Friedenreich et al., pp. 167-91.

15   See David M. Bevington, *From 'Mankind' to Marlowe* (Cambridge, Massachusetts, 1962), pp. 245-62.

16   The play was written between 1400 and 1425. An edition can be found in *Four Morality Plays*, edited by Peter Happé (Harmondsworth, 1979).

17   On the contested notions of grace in the sixteenth century see Robert G. Hunter, *Shakespeare and the Mystery of God's*

Judgments (Athens, Georgia, 1976), pp. 39-66, and Mary Elizabeth Smith, '"Hell Strives with Grace": Reflections on the Theme of Providence in Marlowe', in *The Elizabethan Theatre XI*, edited by A.L. Magnusson and C.E. McGee (Port Credit, 1990), pp. 133-54. Compare King-Kok Cheung, 'The Dialectic of Despair in *Doctor Faustus*', in '*A Poet and a filthy Play-maker*', edited by Friedenreich et al., pp. 193-201.

18 See *Three Late Medieval Morality Plays*, edited by G.A. Lester (London, 1981). It seems likely the play was written about 1520.

19 The speech seems unusually overdetermined, especially in the references to God the father. For psychoanalytic comment see Kuriyama, *Hammer or Anvil*, pp. 95-135, and Frank Ardolino, 'The "Wrath of Frowning Jove": Fathers and Sons in Marlowe's Plays', *Journal of Evolutionary Psychology*, 2 (1981), 83-100.

20 Quoted from *Calvin: Institutes of the Christian Religion* (1559), edited and translated by John T. McNeill and Ford Lewis Battles, Library of Christian Classics, Volumes XX - XXI (London, 1961). The *Institutes* were first printed in 1536.

21 Introduction (1892) to *Socialism: Utopian and Scientific*, in *Karl Marx, Frederick Engels: Collected Works*, Volume XXVII (London, 1990), p. 291. The reference is to Paul's letter to the Romans IX. 16, a locus classicus of calvinist theory. See *Institutes*, II. 5. 4, 17, and III. 24. 1. See also Clarence Green, 'Doctor Faustus: Tragedy of Individualism', *Science and Society*, 10 (1946), 275-83; Ian Watt, 'Faust as a Myth of Modern Individualism: Three of Marlowe's Contributions', in *Faust Through Four Centuries*, edited by Boerner and Johnson, pp. 41-52; and David F. Stover, 'The Individualism of *Doctor Faustus*', *North Dakota Quarterly*, 4 (1989), 146-61.

22 On the sense of election in *Tamburlaine* see Smith, '"Hell Strives with Grace"'. For the view that the later play subverts a calvinist orthodoxy by revealing its harshness see Dollimore,

Radical Tragedy, pp. 109-19; Sinfield, *Literature in
Protestant England*, pp. 116-20; and Keefer, *Doctor Faustus*,
pp. xlv-lv.

Chapter 6: *Hero and Leander*

1   The poem was entered for publication in the stationers'
register on 28 September 1593, and eventually printed in 1598
with a dedication to Thomas Walsingham. *Venus and Adonis*
was most likely written in 1592-3; and printed in 1593,
dedicated to the earl of Southampton. See *William Shakespeare:
The Poems*, edited by F.T. Prince (London, 1960).

2   See *Ovid: Heroides and Amores*, translated by Grant
Showerman (London, 1914), and *Callimachus . . . Musaeus:
Hero and Leander*, edited and translated by C.A. Trypanis,
Thomas Gelzer, and Cedric Whitman, enlarged edition
(Cambridge, Massachusetts, 1978). All reference is to these
editions.

3   For classic critical comment see M.C. Bradbrook, 'Marlowe's
Hero and Leander' (1933), in *Aspects of Dramatic Form in the
English and the Irish Renaissance* (Brighton, 1983), pp. 12-
16, and Steane, *Marlowe*, pp. 302-33.

4   On Marlowe's poem as complete in itself see Marion
Campbell, '"*Desunt Nonnulla*": The Construction of
Marlowe's *Hero and Leander* as an Unfinished Poem', *ELH*,
51 (1984), 241-68.

5   There seems no reason to assume that the narrative viewpoint,
which is offered to the reader for acceptance, is not in effect
Marlowe's. For the contention, nevertheless, that the narrator
is dramatised and unreliable see W.L. Godshalk, '*Hero and
Leander*: The Sense of an Ending', in '*A Poet and a filthy
Play-maker*', edited by Friedenreich et al., pp. 293-314.

6   For a criticism of this moment, however, as essentially
denying the otherness of Hero's sexuality see Cynthia Drew

Hymel, '*Hero and Leander*: A Male Perspective on Female Sexuality', *Journal of Women's Studies in Literature*, 1 (1979), 273-85. A psychoanalytic reading can be found in David Lee Miller, 'The Death of the Modern: Gender and Desire in Marlowe's "Hero and Leander"', *South Atlantic Quarterly*, 88 (1989), 757-87.

7   Ovid enumerates Neptune's lovers, all of them women, in *Heroides*, XIX. 129-40.

8   See *The Compact Edition of the Oxford English Dictionary* (London, 1979), I, 1113, and Smith, *Homosexual Desire in Shakespeare's England*, pp. 191-7.

9   Compare, for instance, the portraits of Elizabeth and court ladies by Nicholas Hilliard in Carl Winter, *Elizabethan Miniatures*, revised edition (Harmondsworth, 1955).

10 The homoeroticism of the description has been noted before: by, for example, Clark Hulse, *Metamorphic Verse: The Elizabethan Minor Epic* (Princeton, New Jersey, 1981), pp. 107-8.

11 A full expression of the ideology of marriage in the sixteenth century can be found in 'The Form of Solemnisation of Matrimony' in the prayer book. See Brightman, *English Rite*, II, 800-17, and the *Book of Common Prayer*, edited by Booty, pp. 290-9.

12 Again, there seems no need effectively to separate the narrative voice from the author's.

13 See Morris Palmer Tilley, *A Dictionary of the Proverbs in England in the Sixteenth and Seventeenth Centuries* (Ann Arbor, 1950), pp. 394-401, and *Callimachus . . . Musaeus,* edited by Trypanis et al., pp. 310-11, 356-7.

14 Compare, for example, Spenser's *Prothalamion*, ll. 5-10, 137-42, which he wrote in 1596, in *Spenser: Selected Writings*, edited by Elizabeth Porges Watson (London, 1992).

15 On the concepts mobilised in this paragraph see *Developing Contemporary Marxism*, edited by Zygmunt G. Baranski and

John R. Short (London, 1985), especially the essays by Paul Corner, John Urry, Patrick Dunleavy, Giulio Lepschy, Zygmunt G. Baranski, and Bob Lumley and Michael O'Shaughnessey, pp. 89-164, 199-292; and *Marxism and the Interpretation of Culture*, edited by Cary Nelson and Lawrence Grossberg (London, 1988), in particular their introduction, pp. 1-13.

Index

Abiram, 23

Absalom, 23-4

Absolutism, 20, 54, 57, 61, 75, 100

Adam, 68

Agriculture, 39

America, 15

Anticapitalism, 40, 41-3, 46, 49, 57, 98

Anticatholicism, 21-3, 62-4

Antifeudalism, 44-6, 51, 57

Antisemitism, 33-4, 36-7, 40, 41-3, 97

Antwerp, 40, 41

Aristocracy, feudal, 44, 46, 48, 49, 56

Armada, 14, 38, 63, 94

Asia, 14

Audience, 17-18, 22, 36, 39, 40, 41, 58, 64, 69, 76, 95, 96

Bacon family, 48

Bacon, Francis, 68; *New Atlantis*, 102

Baines, Richard, 12

Bairseth, 41

Bakeless, John, 11

Baldock, Robert, 47

Bible, 23, 41, 68, 73, 96, 97; Exodus, 27; Genesis, 69, 79; Leviticus, 59, 86. See also Matthew, Luke, Paul

Bologna, 65

Book of Common Prayer, 13, 105

Bourbon, Henry, 62-4

Bourgeoisie, 64, 75, 76, 90

Bradley, William, 12

Bruno, Giordano, 66-7

Bull, Eleanor, 12

Burghley, Lord. See William Cecil

Cabot, John, 15

Calvin, John, *Institutes of the Christian Religion*, 74, 103

Calvinism, 74-5, 103-4

Cambridge, 11-12
Canterbury, 11, 12
Capitalism, 21, 39, 40, 41-3, 52, 57, 75, 90, 96, 98; financial, 40, 42-3; international, 40-1; landed, 43; mercantile, 39-42, 43; rise of, 13, 17, 39, 42
Catholicism, 12, 14, 21-3, 62, 63, 96
Cavendish family, 48
Cecil family, 48
Cecil, William, 12, 41
Chancellor, Richard, 15
Charles V, emperor, 42
Charles IX, 62
Cheshire, 48
China, 15
Chislehurst, 12
Christ, Jesus, 22-3, 33, 42, 68, 74
Christianity, 21, 23, 34, 37, 72, 74
Cicero, 60
Class, 11, 17-18, 44, 46-9, 61, 64, 90, 95; fraction, 90; ruling, 17, 29, 44, 48, 62, 64
Clément, Jacques, 63
Coalmining, 39
Colonisation, 15
Commodity fetishism, 39
Condensation, 18
Copernicanism, 66-7

Copernicus, Nicolaus. See Kopernik, Mikolaj
Corkine, William, 12
Corpus Christi College, Cambridge,11
Coultras, battle of, 63
Court, 56, 64, 105
Cracow, 65
Cromwell, Oliver, 16
Culture, 13, 43, 93, 102

Dathan, 23
David, 24
Dee, John, 66-7, 102
Dekker, Thomas, *Shoemaker's Holiday*, 43, 99
Denmark, 53
Deptford, 12
Desire, 59, 67, 81-3, 86, 87
Despenser, Hugh le, 48
Dialogism, 16
Digges, Thomas, 66-7
Discourse, 16, 17, 21, 25, 28, 30, 32, 33-4, 36, 40, 47, 48-9, 54-5, 59, 63, 65, 66-7, 76, 86, 95, 97; dominant, 19-20, 23-4, 38, 45-6, 59, 68-71. See also Ideology
Displacement, 14, 29, 37, 41-3, 46, 53, 64, 90
Donne, John, 11, 12, 17-18, 48, 100; 'Sun Rising', 95
Drake, Francis, 15

Education, 11, 14, 47, 48, 76; secularisation of, 13
Edward II, 53, 56-7
Edward III, 56-7
Effacement, 42, 44
Egerton, Thomas, 48
Elizabeth I, 11, 12, 13, 14, 18, 20, 25, 29, 30, 45, 48, 53, 60, 63-4, 90, 94, 95, 102, 105
Empedocles, 79
Engels, Frederick, *Socialism: Utopian and Scientific*, 75, 103
England, 13, 14, 18, 37-8, 41, 48, 53, 56-7, 63-4, 66-7, 102
Ermland, 65
Europe, 13, 14, 32-3, 37, 39, 40-2; eastern, 21-2, 40-1
Eve, 68

Faustus, Georgius Sabellicus, junior. See George Helmstetter
Feild, John, 66-7
Ferrara, 65
Feudalism, 46, 51, 57, 72, 90-1, 96; decline of, 13, 17, 48; ideology of, 13, 17, 40, 47-8, 74, 95, 98
Florence, 40
Flushing, 12
France, 47, 60, 62, 64
Frankfurt, 40

Frauenburg, 65
Frizer, Ingram, 12
Frobisher, Martin, 15
Fugger family, 41, 42

Galilei, Galileo, 66
'Ganymede', 81, 85
Gascony, 47
Gaveston, Piers, 47, 57
Gender, 20, 46, 61, 86-7
Gentry, 11, 46-7, 48
Germany, 41, 64-5
Government, 11, 37-8, 53
Grace, 72-3, 102-3
Gresham, Thomas, 41-2
Guise, duke of. See Henry of Lorraine

Hassfurt, Johannes Virdung von, 101
Heidelberg, 64
Heliocentrism, 65, 66-7
Helmstadt, 64
Helmstetter, George, 64-6, 101
Henry III, king of France, 62, 63-4
Henry IV, king of France. See Henry Bourbon
Henry VIII, 14, 15, 42, 48
Herod, 31
Hierarchy, 20, 45-6, 53, 61, 75, 77, 79, 86
Hilliard, Nicholas, 105

History, 14, 16, 17, 29, 30, 32-3, 34-5, 38, 41, 42, 44, 47, 48, 51, 52, 53, 55, 56-7, 58-9, 60, 62, 64, 65-6, 69-70, 71, 74, 75, 93, 94, 98

History of the Damnable Life and Deserved Death of Doctor John Faustus, 65-6, 68, 71, 74, 101

Holinshed, Raphael, *Chronicles*, 44, 47, 52, 53, 55, 57-9, 99

Homilies, 13; 'Against Disobedience', 23-4; 'Against Whoredom and Uncleanness', 59; 'Of Obedience', 19-20, 23-4

Homosexuality, 57, 59-61, 62, 63, 81-5, 86, 87, 89, 91, 94, 100, 105

Hooker, Richard, *Laws of Ecclesiastical Polity*, 68, 102

Humanism, 11, 13, 14, 24, 30, 31, 44, 65, 68, 76, 94

Hungary, 21

Hutten, Moritz von, 101

Hutten, Philip von, 65, 101

Idealism, 68

Ideology, 19, 21, 30, 38, 40, 60, 61, 73, 74-5, 95; dominant, 13, 20, 24, 27, 30, 51, 52, 53, 54, 85-7, 90-1. See also Discourse

Imperialism, 13, 14, 15, 18-19, 21, 30, 37, 98

Incorporation, 12, 21, 29

Individualism, 11, 19-21, 30, 38, 48-9, 51, 52-3, 56-7, 61, 62, 74-5, 90-1, 95

Industry, 39

Inns of Court, 48

Interest, 42-3

Interiority, 50-1, 52

Intertextuality, 31, 33, 40, 47, 51, 52, 55, 58-9, 65-6, 68, 72, 74, 76, 98

Ipswich, 48

Ireland, 53; conquest and settlement of, 15-16, 53

Islam, 21, 37

James I, 48, 95, 100

Jews, 32-3, 38-9, 41, 42

Job, 33

Joyeuse, Anne de, 62

Kepler, Johann, 66

King's School, Canterbury, 11

Kopernik, Mikolaj, 65-6, 101; *On the Revolutions of the Heavenly Spheres*, 65, 67, 101

Korah, 23

Koran, 23

Lennox, duke of. See Esmé Stuart

London, 12, 21, 22, 40, 41, 64, 76

Lorraine, Henry of, 62
Lübeck, 41
Luke, 42
Luther, Martin, 65

Machiavelli, Niccolò, 31, 32, 40; *Prince*, 35, 97
Machiavellianism, 31-7, 40, 43
Malta, 37-8; knights of, 35, 38; siege of, 38
Marlowe, Christopher, 17-18, 29, 37, 41, 47, 48, 64, 69, 94; *Doctor Faustus*, 62, 64-75, 85, 90, 91; *Edward II*, 44-61, 62, 85, 90-1; *Hero and Leander*, 76-91; *Jew of Malta*, 31-43, 44, 50, 64, 90; life, 11-13; *Massacre at Paris,* 62-4; *Tamburlaine*, Part I, 14-21, 24, 25, 38, 47, 48-50, 51, 52-3, 56, 64, 75, 85, 90-1; Part II, 21-30, 34, 35, 37, 38, 48-9, 51, 52-3, 55, 64, 90
Marriage, 18-19, 86-7; ideology of, 59, 86, 105
Mary I, 13
Mary, queen of Scots, 48
Matthew, 33, 40
Maugiron, François de, 62
Medici, Catherine de, 62
Mediterranean, 14
Middle ages, 42

Mobility, social, 11, 17-18, 47-9, 59, 61, 62, 64, 69-70
Monarchy, 13, 20, 43, 44, 45-6, 48, 49, 52, 53-7, 61, 62, 63, 75, 86, 90-1, 99-100
Monastic land, 41
Moneylending, 42-3
Mongolia, 14
Morality plays, 31, 35, 72, 74; *Castle of Perseverance*, 72, 73, 102; *Everyman*, 73, 103
More, Thomas, *Utopia*, 39, 98
Moscow, 41
Munster, colonisation of, 15
Murad II, 96
Musaeus, *Hero and Leander*, 76-7, 80, 81, 84, 86, 87-8, 89-90
Mystery plays, 31
Myth, 56-7, 60, 66, 76, 87, 96

Nationalism, 21, 62; rise of, 13
Naturalism, 39, 50
Newgate, 12
Nunez, Hector, 41

Octavian, 60
O'Neill, Hugh, 53
Overdetermination, 103
Ovid, *Heroides*, 76, 77, 79, 81, 82-3, 89, 105; *Metamorphoses*, 51
Oxford, 48

Padua, 65
Papacy, 21, 22, 62-3
Papermills, 41
Parliament, 59; rise of, 13
Patronage, 11, 12, 76, 90
Paul, Colossians, 68; 1
    Corinthians, 59, 68;
    Romans, 103
Perondini, Pietro, *Life* of
    Tamburlaine, 14, 16, 17,
    29
Plato, 89
Poland, 65, 96
Policy, 31-7
Predestination, 75, 103
Prester John, 21
Privy council, 12, 20-1
Protestantism, 14, 18, 22, 62-
    4, 71, 74, 96; rise of, 13
Ptolemaic universe, 67

Radicalism, 21, 28, 30, 61,
    85-7, 90-1
Ramée, Pierre de la, 62
Ramus, Petrus. See Pierre de
    la Ramée
Rebellion, northern, 23-4
Recorde, Robert, 66-7
Reformation, 14
Renaissance, 14, 31, 66, 76,
    84, 102
Revolution, English, 94
Revolution, scientific, 68, 101
Rhodes, siege of, 35
Rome, 12, 21-2, 65

Royal Exchange, 41
Russell family, 48
Russia company, 41

Satan, 69
Satire, 49
Scadbury, 12
Science, 65, 66-7, 70-1, 73-4,
    102; rise of, 13, 65, 66,
    68, 101
Self-projection, 17-18, 47, 62,
    95
Seville, 40
Sexuality, 57-9, 78-81, 84, 86-
    90, 104-5
Seymour family, 48
Shakespeare, William, 11, 12,
    17-18, 99-100; *Venus and
    Adonis*, 76, 104
Shoreditch, 12
Sigismund III, 96
Southampton, earl of. See
    Henry Wriothesley
Spain, 12, 13, 14, 15, 37, 38,
    62-3, 94
Spenser, Edmund, 78; *Faerie
    Queene*, 18; *Prothalamion*,
    105
State, 12, 60; centralisation of,
    13, 53, 55
Stoicism, 23-8, 30, 90, 96
Stow, John, *Chronicles*, 55
Stuart, Esmé, 100
Subversion, 20, 21, 30, 79, 87,
    99-100

Succession, 28-9, 55
Suicide, 27-8

Tamburlaine, 14, 16-17, 29
Torun, 65
Trade, 39, 40
Transgression, 27-8
Trithemius, Johannes, 68, 101
Tudors, 48
Turkey, 14, 35, 37, 38, 94
Tyburn, 52

Usury, 42
Utopianism, 68

Valois, Margaret, 62
Varna, battle of, 96
Venezuela, 65
Venice, 40
Vice, 31, 32, 39, 43, 59, 97
Virginia, 15
Vladislav III, 96

Wager, William, *Enough Is as
    Good as a Feast*, 31, 37, 98
Walsingham, Francis, 11, 21,
    38, 63
Walsingham, Thomas, 11, 12,
    104
Watson, Thomas, 12
Whetstone, George, *English
    Mirror*, 14, 16, 17, 29-30
Willoughby, Hugh, 15
Wolsey, Thomas, 48
Wriothesley, Henry, 104